PUZZLES WITH
PAPER &
CARDBOARD

PUZZLES WITH PAPER & CARDBOARD

Jack Botermans

Text: Rob van den Dobbelsteen
Photography: David van Dijk
Models: Jeannet Leendertse

David & Charles

First published in the UK by David & Charles 1986
© Translation David & Charles 1986
© 1985 Planned and produced by Plenary Publications International
(Europe bv), Amsterdam and ADM International bv, Amsterdam

British Library Cataloguing in Publication Data.
Botermans, Jack
Puzzles with paper and cardboard
1. Puzzles
I. Title
793.73   GV1493

ISBN 0-7153-8860-6

Printed in The Netherlands
for David & Charles Publishers plc Brunel House Newton Abbot Devon

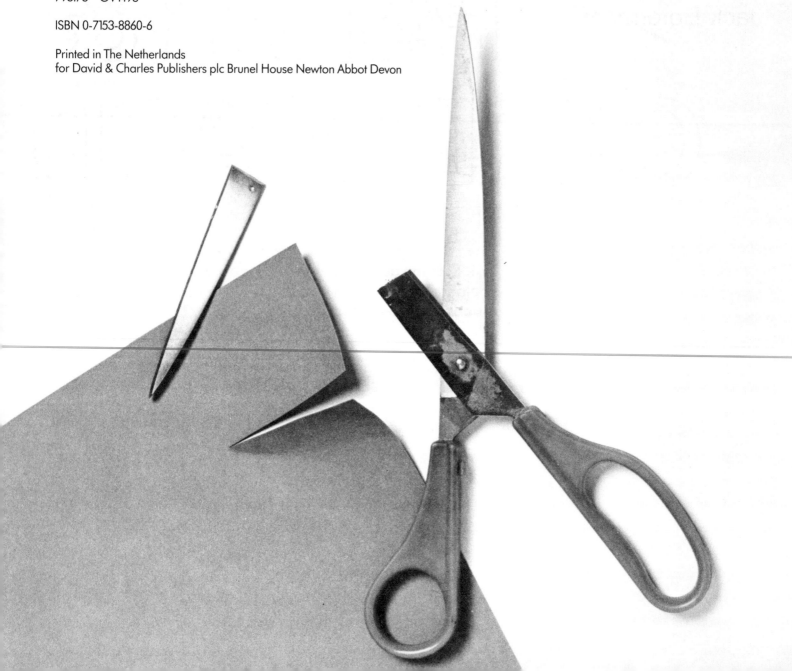

CONTENTS

INTRODUCTION

Paper is one of the most commonly used materials in daily life. Man has been using paper for thousands of years, and as yet it has not been replaced by any other material.

In the year 3000 BC the Egyptians were writing on the bark of the Papyrus plant and they continued to do so for the next four thousand years. The actual invention of paper as we know it is generally attributed to the Chinese in the second century AD.

The importance of paper for the purposes of communication and the dissemination of knowledge is obvious, and this aspect became even more widespread with the invention of printing.

In many societies paper has also acquired an essential role in cultural expression and as an artistic medium for local traditions.

For example, paper cut-out patterns from Poland are well known for their vitality and imagination and are considered as a form of folk art.

In Mexico, paper is used in many festive celebrations to make bunting, pinatas and numerous other cardboard and paper constructions which are used in colourful processions.

In Japan, paper was used for many different purposes, partly from economic necessity and partly for traditional reasons. Paper can be an effective material and it is cheap and generally easily available. The inherently sensitive nature of Japanese people has produced a variety of paper articles which are remarkable for their artistic quality as well as for their sense of humour. The art of paper folding is a favourite pastime of both children and adults in Japan.

Many years ago the art of making silhouettes was stimulated by monasteries throughout Europe. Today there is a revival of the creative use of paper in Western Europe, following the Japanese example. There are shops specialising in paper equipment, selling beautiful kites, for example. Not only the practical aspects of paper are considered, but also the ways in which it can be used as a hobby.

This book by Jack Botermans shows how paper and its rather coarser brother, cardboard, have provided endless pleasure for many people. It is about the elevated art of making something from virtually nothing, something attractive or amusing or surprising. The artistic element depends largely on your skill and dexterity, and all the models and toys in this book are a fascinating challenge. The book is aimed at those who are passionate about DIY, who need only a sheet of paper or a piece of cardboard to cut up – plus a pair of scissors or a Stanley knife – to turn a dream into a reality. The reality will be fantastic objects created from next to nothing: a floating pyramid, strange dice, magnificent 3-d stars, and puzzles both ancient and modern – with objects like these, you enter the realms of magic.

TOOLS AND MATERIALS

What sort of paper is best to use, and what tools do you need? These are important questions and we will attempt to answer them below.

Paper

You will need a number of different sorts of paper. Obviously no one will mind if you simply tear a sheet off the nearest pad of paper, but there are many different kinds you can use. Not only the thickness of the paper is important, but also the actual structure. Paper can have a rough surface, it can be transparent or veined. Thus the type of paper you use depends on what you are going to do with it. With regard to the strength of your construction, it goes without saying that this depends to a great extent on the quality of paper you use. Always remember this.

Tools

For most of the objects described in this book you need only a few household tools or kitchen and garden implements. You won't have to buy any special equipment, though some people might consider that a stapler falls into this category. However, if you don't have a stapler, ordinary pins will do just as well. Pegs or paperclips are used to hold the glued surfaces together while the glue dries, and you will need scissors of various types and sizes. There is a wide variety of sellotape, Stanley knives and glue. In most cases you will find all these in the home, and when you start to build the models described in this book you will only need to go shopping for the actual paper, perhaps some paint and... this book. It really couldn't be cheaper.

This page shows a number of the tools you will need to make the models described in this book:

Ruler
Scissors
Stanley knife
Blunt potato knife (for scoring lines)
Pencils and crayons
Felt tips
Stapler
Paperclips
Pins
Clothes pegs
Sellotape

With a simple twisting movement, fold a piece of card into an impossible object.

THE IMPOSSIBLE OBJECT 1

This idea is rather like a joke which is suddenly being told everywhere, in pubs and cafés throughout the land, in cities and country villages, though no one has any idea who told it first or where it originated.

This is rather unfortunate for the person who first thought of the joke – always assuming that it was a good one – for even if he got only a penny each time it was told, he would be able to retire on it.

In fact these 'impossible constructions' created with little bits of paper are very similar. Who thought of them first? Perhaps a father trying to impress his sons by making an impossible sculpture using no more than a piece of card folded and cut in an extremely ingenious way. This might be the answer, but there's really no way of finding out the truth. These creations simply suddenly appeared to amuse both those who were making them and those who merely stood around watching.

It's certainly advisable for a beginner to use card which has a pattern or structure on it so that you can camouflage the folds and cuts more easily.

A Stanley knife can be used to score the lines of the folds first, and this is an essential tool for anyone making these structures.

When you have cut the centre piece, as in this example, and scored along the lines, the model can be folded into the right shape by simply turning it on its axis. It may be simple, but at the same time it's very puzzling.

To make the construction look even more puzzling you must camouflage the places where the folded cardboard comes together as much as you can. This can be done by decorating the construction or otherwise by rubbing out the cut slightly with a blunt object.

If you wish to perfect the actual presentation of your 'impossible' structure, it can be placed under a glass dome or in a perspex box so that no one can touch it.

This round model forms an interesting variation on the rectangular 'miracle'. It is always possible to camouflage the cuts.

A WORK OF ART CONSISTING OF TETRAHEDRA

We will begin by explaining exactly what a tetrahedron is, as you might be under the impression that this term refers to a recently discovered tribe originating from the heart of darkest Africa. This is certainly not the case. As any mathematician will tell you, a tetrahedron is a regular structure which consists of four equilateral triangles.

The strip of card shown at the bottom of the following page consists of ten of these tetrahedra. This is a very special strip, as you will soon see if you examine it carefully.

You can twist the circle which can be made from this strip around its own axis to produce an extremely interesting effect, especially when the strip is painted in different bright colours.

This is merely one of the many possibilities. Obviously you don't need to make exactly ten tetrahedra – eight will do just as well, though this evidently restricts the possibilities to some extent. However, it's just as much fun making one of these special circles with ten as with eight tetrahedra.

Of course, you could always make a circle with twenty tetrahedra. This is even more fun because it means you can make a knot in the strip to produce a wonderful sight when you play around with the circle. The strips are very suitable for use as a bracelet or to give someone as a present, but a really ingenious person could use this standard model to make an extremely original work of art. There are plenty of possibilities to work with.

To make a ring of ten tetrahedra you need a piece of card 40 × 10 cm with an approximate thickness of 0.25 mm. The card should be folded meticulously. First score the lines with a Stanley knife. When you have cut everything out and scored all the lines as shown in the diagram, fold along the lines, bending the card forwards and backwards a few times. The order of sticking down the tabs can be seen from the numbering, ie, stick No 1 down on No 1, No 2 on No 2, and so on. Remember that this should be done very accurately as otherwise you will end up with a disaster. Obviously the way in which you decorate the circle, by painting it or gluing decorations on, is entirely up to you. The more colourful your circle is, the more exciting it will look.

This flat strip of card is transformed with a few folds and some glue into a genuine work of art.

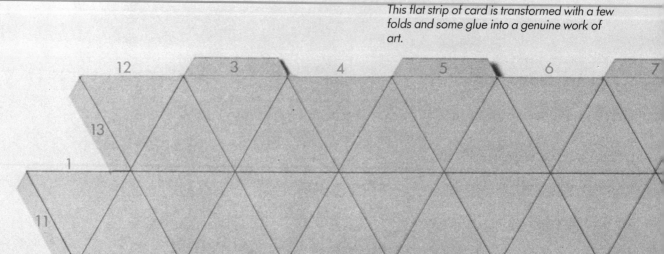

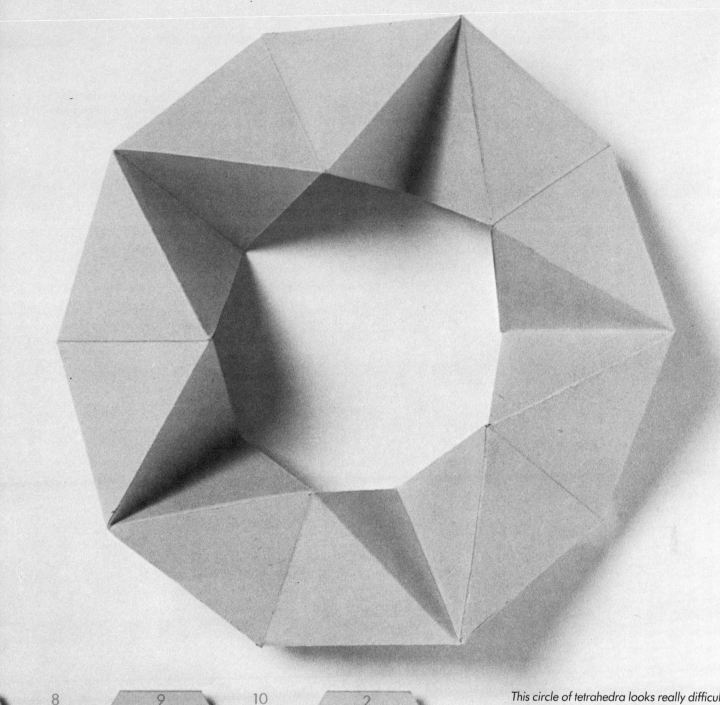

This circle of tetrahedra looks really difficult to make, but you will see that it is actually fairly simple.
Moreover, you won't be the only one to be surprised by the results — all your friends will be impressed as well.

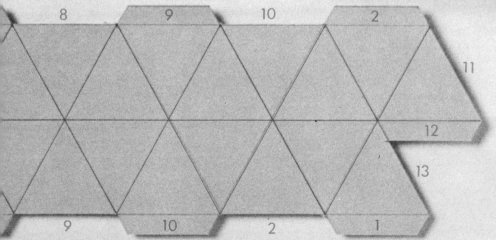

The cube will snap shut with considerable force. This may give the person receiving it rather a shock but this is soon followed by a lovely surprise.

A SNAPPER

Here comes the postman bringing a mysterious parcel wrapped in brown paper. What a surprise and what fun to send someone a surprise like this. They'll wonder if it's a box of chocolates or possibly a book ordered so long ago that they've forgotten all about it.

They try and undo the knots in the string with impatient fingers, nervously tear the tough wrapping paper when suddenly... The mysterious thing they wonderingly unwrapped snaps shut and a cube appears in their hands. This could bear some sort of original message from the sender or the notification of a change of address, an invitation to a birthday party or New Year best wishes. If you want to make your own snapper and you want to make sure that your message is read, you could make your own cube, for example, one decorated with photographs of yourself and your family or with your own drawings. Don't imagine for a moment that a cube like this is difficult to make — it's actually very straightforward.

To make a cube 9 × 9 × 9 cm you need a piece of card 27 cm wide by 48 cm long. Make sure that the card is at least 0.75 mm thick. Copy the design shown here onto the piece of card. Cut out or cut the model and score the lines which need folding with the blunt edge of a pair of scissors or with a blunt potato knife. The whole model is stuck together as shown in the second example.

The tube on one side of the structure gives additional strength to the design. The most difficult part of the exercise is the next step, which can be rather fiddly, though an ordinary elastic band will be a great help. Finish by showing the message on the cube, and there you are!

These two stages show how this snapper cube is made.

A FLEXICUBE

Inventors are extraordinary people. When looking for one thing they often end up unexpectedly inventing something totally different. Mr A.H. Stone, an English mathematician who was studying in the United States, was someone like this. He was researching equilateral triangles made of flexible material when he chanced upon the cube described in this chapter.

Stone immediately realised the attractive aspects of this puzzle, for by chance he had managed to turn it inside out completely without using so much as a pair of scissors or a pot of glue. Then he wondered whether the average puzzler would be able to do this too.

It soon became obvious that the average person certainly couldn't manage this and the odd individual who did succeed took quite a long time over it. The flexicube turned out to be quite a complicated puzzle which made great demands on anyone keen on puzzles, let alone a complete amateur.

Obviously you can make the flexicube of paper or card, and if we were strictly adhering to the title of this book it certainly should be made of paper, but there is no reason why another material shouldn't be used. For example, this puzzle is very attractive when made of tin joined together on the inside with sellotape in such a way that there is enough room to fold between the corners. If you find this difficult to follow, there is a diagram showing the simple construction of a flexicube made of card or paper.

To make the flexicube, use a strip of card approximately 8 × 23 cm. Copy all the lines shown in the diagram onto this card. Now score along all these lines with a Stanley knife. To make a really flexible, easy-to-manipulate flexicube it is a good idea to bend the card backwards and forwards along these lines a few times.

Before sticking the strip of card into the shape of a cube with sellotape, it is advisable to give the sides of the cube a particular colour. This depends entirely on your own taste – a bright red, a subdued blue, a glaring yellow – whatever you like best. The coloured sides make it easier to see later on whether you have really succeeded in turning the flexicube inside out. This might otherwise be rather doubtful.

Before we go on to the next example and forget to tell you how to turn the flexicube inside out, this is how to do it: first press the two corners A together to form a flat square in which – as shown in the illustration – the bottom corners are also folded towards each other (1). Then fold corners B towards each other to make a triangle (2). A square is produced when you then press in the corners C (3). Now pull out point D and fold the whole thing flat. Do the same with point D at the back of figure 4. You are now exactly halfway, so don't give up. Make another flat square and fold the corners E in (5). Turn the square around and pull the corners D out to make another flat square.

Now pull it all open – there you are. You can put everything back in its original form by reversing the process.

This, plus some sellotape is all you need to make this puzzle.

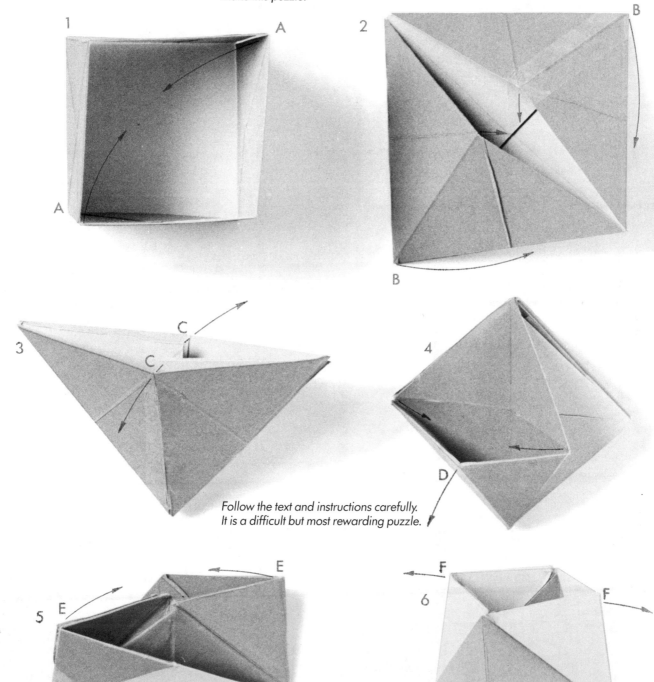

Follow the text and instructions carefully. It is a difficult but most rewarding puzzle.

In his 'Encyclopaedia of Puzzles', which dates from 1914, Sam Lloyd calls this puzzle 'a royal success'. There are three solutions to it including Lloyd's own.

THE DIVIDED CHESSBOARD

At first sight this divided chessboard looks very simple; a puzzle which you would imagine could be solved in a few seconds. However appearances are deceptive. Researching the background to this puzzle, Jerry Slocum, who compiled a short book of chess puzzles, came across a remarkable quotation by a certain Professor Hoffman.

In 1893 this scientist had already warned against the deceptive simplicity of the solution of this puzzle, 'until you find that you have space left for only three pieces, while you are still holding six in your hands...' Quite possibly Hoffman spent many fruitless evenings attempting to solve the mystery of this puzzle with its double bottom.

Slocum also discovered that a patent had been taken out on the puzzle in September 1880 for the United States of America. The person taking out this patent was Henry Buers, who considered that the puzzle was such a pleasant way of whiling away long winter evenings that this was in itself a good enough reason for popularising it.

Buers probably thought that he'd struck gold – like those who invented Scrabble and Monopoly – but this turned out to be a disappointment, probably because the divided chessboard was too easy to make.

Take a piece of cardboard approximately 16 cm square and draw a chequered pattern on it with squares 2 × 2 cm. To make it look like a chessboard the squares are coloured alternately black and white. Obviously you can use felt tips to do this, but a more professional look is usually obtained if you stick pieces of black paper on every other square. Then you cut out the pieces in the pattern shown here. This is based on eight pieces, but there is absolutely no reason why you should not make your own version. If you do this you must assume that fifteen pieces is the maximum number for an attractive puzzle. To make it a little easier, you could also make a little box about 16 × 16 cm with the chequered pattern drawn onto it.

You can make a number of different versions of the Divided Chessboard. This is the version with thirteen pieces, designed by Gary Foshee.

THE MOBIUS STRIP

The Mobius strip is a miracle of simplicity named after Augustus Mobius, a German mathematician from the last century. The whole puzzle is no more than a piece of paper with one cut in it. The stroke of genius consists in the way it is twisted and the way in which the ends of the strip are stuck together (the bottom onto the top). You can no longer tell which is the inside and which is the outside. They seem to simply merge together.

The Mobius strip isn't used just to fascinate the audience. Try experimenting with it yourself and you'll be surprised by the results.

There is nothing so simple to make as a Mobius strip, but you must begin by deciding what sort you want to make. The easiest is a strip of paper with a cut down the middle. Then twist the strip through 360° and stick the ends together so that the top is stuck onto the bottom. With a bit of cutting you will find that you end up with two links of a chain entwined together.

However, this is not the only possibility. Provided the strip is long enough, it is possible to give it an extra twist, or just to twist it through 180°. If you now stick the ends together the effect is even stranger. This also applies to the strip with a cut which is not quite in the middle so that it has a wide and a narrow half.

Another nice idea is to use two Mobius strips together. If you then twist them and stick the ends together the results will be different again. There are countless possibilities with the Mobius strip, some of which are quite unpredictable. For example, if you colour the halves in different colours, you will be delighted with the effect, which has an almost magical quality. This is even further enhanced when you use a number of strips with half twists as well as whole and double twists. It's not for nothing that conjurors wax lyrical about the possibilities of the magical Mobius strip.

UNKNOWN UPHILL FORCES

Surely this isn't possible? If you think that, you're wrong. This cone seems to roll uphill, as though one of the works of the graphic artist M.C. Escher has come to life. In his drawings Escher even managed to suggest that water could flow uphill. This cone, which rolls uphill, is perhaps not quite as spectacular, but nevertheless...

Perhaps it isn't really rolling uphill. Is it an optical illusion, just like Escher's work? The truth of the matter is that it is, and the observer is taken for a ride. If you look closely, you will see that in reality the cone is rolling downhill. The strange 'track', the triangle on which the cone rolls, as well as the cone itself, are so sophisticated that the cone seems to roll uphill.

You could compare it to a mountain road. When you have gone up for a while, on your bike, or, in greater comfort, in your car, you will notice just before you get to the top that the road seems to run down again. This is an illusion, and if you then decide to shift into neutral gear, you will see that you will start rolling back down.

The phenomenon never ceases to amaze, just like the cone.

The cone consists of two separate cones stuck together and made as shown in the diagram below. To ensure that it will roll smoothly, the lip which serves to stick the two parts together, should not be folded. You must first score along the indented side of the cone with a Stanley knife to make a really sharp angle. The two cones can then be stuck together along this indented edge.

The track which the cone rolls 'up' is made of a strip of card. You must do this exactly in accordance with the sizes given, otherwise the 'illusion' will not work. Lastly, although the examples in this book are always made with paper and card, as the title suggests, there is no reason why this cone, which rolls uphill, should not be made of wood. However, in this case it should be turned wood, and this is not as easy for an amateur to produce. All the same, it's certainly worthwhile making an attempt.

The sides of these figures should be followed exactly.

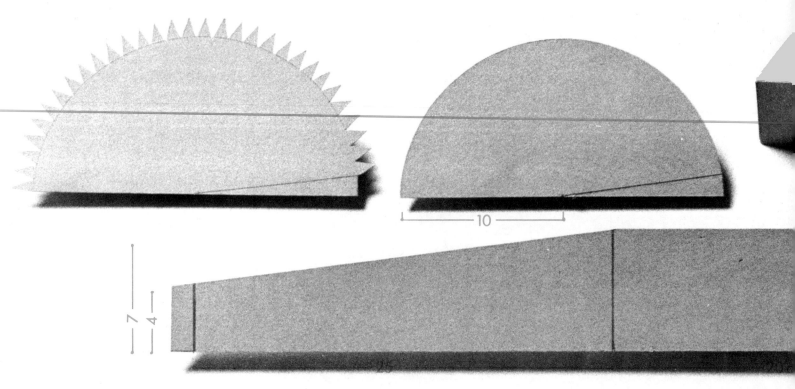

It looks like a solution to the energy problem. You won't believe your eyes when you see the cone rolling uphill under its own steam.

Onlookers will stare in wonder and incredulity.
How is it possible? This is the impossible
made real.

24

THE IMPOSSIBLE OBJECT 2

You won't believe your eyes and you'll find yourself staring at something quite impossible for minutes on end, your forehead wrinkled in incomprehension. The more you turn it round and round, the more difficult it is to understand. Higher forces must have been at work. Perhaps the work of the Great Magician himself.

If you want to be the star attraction at any party, this is the birthday present to give, preferably presented in a sturdy perspex box which is impossible to open. Superglue is the ideal adhesive for this purpose. Your present will undoubtedly be the main talking point of the evening and you will find that everyone will want to know the secret of this 'impossible' object.

The secret lies mainly in the legerdemain which is so popular amongst conjurors. No matter how carefully you look, you can't see everything. For example, you can't see the places where the card has been cut, or was it folded, or where the cuts merge into folds, or are they really just cuts?

Obviously it requires extreme accuracy to make this impossible object, but once you've completed it, you'll find you can't wait to do another.

Of course, it's always possible to make this impossible object from a business card that someone's just given you. You'll find that this is always a great success.

But if it's the first time that you're trying one, it's best to make a slightly larger model. On the other hand, don't make one of giant proportions or an observant onlooker will soon be able to fathom the secret.

It's a good idea to start with an 'impossible object' measuring about 15 × 15 cm. Use card roughly 0.5 mm thick and try to find card which has the same sort of surface on both sides. This surface, like the decoration you can add later, makes it even more possible to trick the observer and to hide the secret cuts and folds in such a way that they are invisible to the human eye.

Carefully follow the three examples given below and erase any guidelines you have drawn. If you have a pair of folding scissors, this is obviously an advantage in making one of these 'eyecatchers' from a business card.

MOVING HOUSE

Have you ever moved house? If not, don't start now because there's nothing as depressing as moving house. It can drive you quite crazy. One minute you can be holding a valuable vase in your hand, the next it has disappeared. General panic follows. You can't remember whether it's actually in the removal van, or where exactly – it might even still be in the attic with the other junk. It all leads to quarrelling and remarks like: 'Why don't you think when you put things down?' In other words, moving house is one of the worst things that can happen to you. However, this certainly isn't true of the moving house puzzle, which is really good fun. Although it won't come as a great surprise that the man who first dreamed up this puzzle, J.H. Flemming, was once a removal man. No one else could have thought of such a thing. You really have to have a streak of the devil in you to come up with this one.

Just imagine that you have a living-room and in this living-room there is a grand piano. This has undoubtedly been the most unpopular article of furniture with removal men since Stan Laurel and Oliver Hardy dragged one down a steep flight of stairs. Fortunately the piano in this puzzle doesn't have to leave the room. Once you've got it in the door, you've succeeded in doing the puzzle. However, this is not so simple, as there is quite a bit of furniture in the room already. As all the other articles of furniture are just as heavy as the piano, and you are quite alone, you'll have to do a fair bit of rearranging. The cupboard can go in the corner and the piano comes forward. Then the piano can be moved further forward still, so that the cupboard can go behind it, and this will make some room for the table. Or might it be better to put the table there so that the chair can be moved to the right? Or perhaps there's another more sensible way of doing it. You'll soon realize that it can drive you completely round the twist, just like moving house can, but at least you'll never lose anything when doing this moving house puzzle – we hope.

The moving house puzzle is fairly easy to make yourself. You'll need two pieces of card. The card should be at least 2 mm thick. The first piece is used to make a box representing the room, and the second piece of card (24 × 29 cm) is used to make the furniture, as shown in the diagram.

It's a good idea to round off the corners of the furniture by filing them with a nail file. This means they will be easier to slide past each other. Label the pieces so that you know what each represents, or stick a picture on each piece of furniture concerned. More creative people can

A good training for anyone who's contemplating moving house: the moving house puzzle.

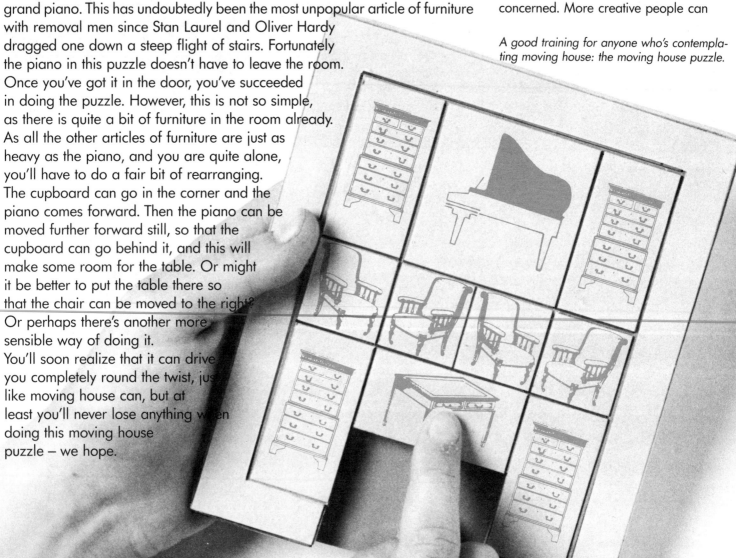

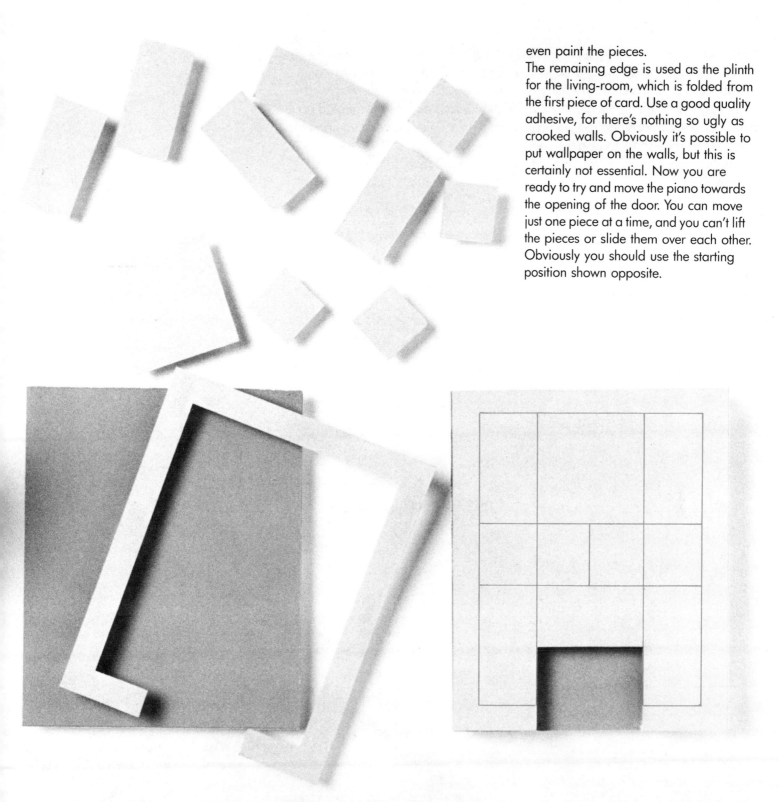

even paint the pieces.

The remaining edge is used as the plinth for the living-room, which is folded from the first piece of card. Use a good quality adhesive, for there's nothing so ugly as crooked walls. Obviously it's possible to put wallpaper on the walls, but this is certainly not essential. Now you are ready to try and move the piano towards the opening of the door. You can move just one piece at a time, and you can't lift the pieces or slide them over each other. Obviously you should use the starting position shown opposite.

The edge of the piece of card used to cut out the pieces of furniture can serve as the plinth for the living-room where the removal takes place.

Just for fun, it's possible to draw the articles of furniture concerned on your pieces.

CATCHING THE SWAN

You'll sometimes come across a dogcatcher in early American cartoons:
a rather dopey figure driving around in a dilapidated van with an assortment
of nets. But the dogcatchers in American cartoons don't seem to do very well.
Either they are bitten on the backside by giant bulldogs or they get tangled up
in their own enormous nets. So we have chosen a far safer piece of equipment
– a sliding cage – to try to trap a swan.
This sliding cage is easy to make yourself and the swan can be folded in the
origami style.

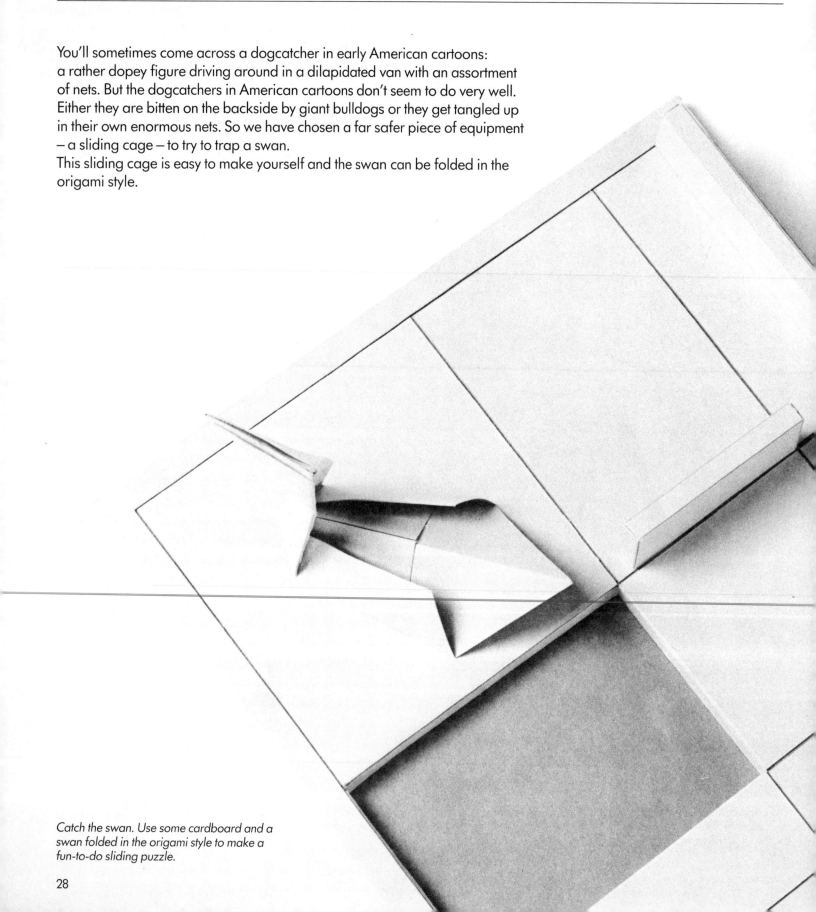

*Catch the swan. Use some cardboard and a
swan folded in the origami style to make a
fun-to-do sliding puzzle.*

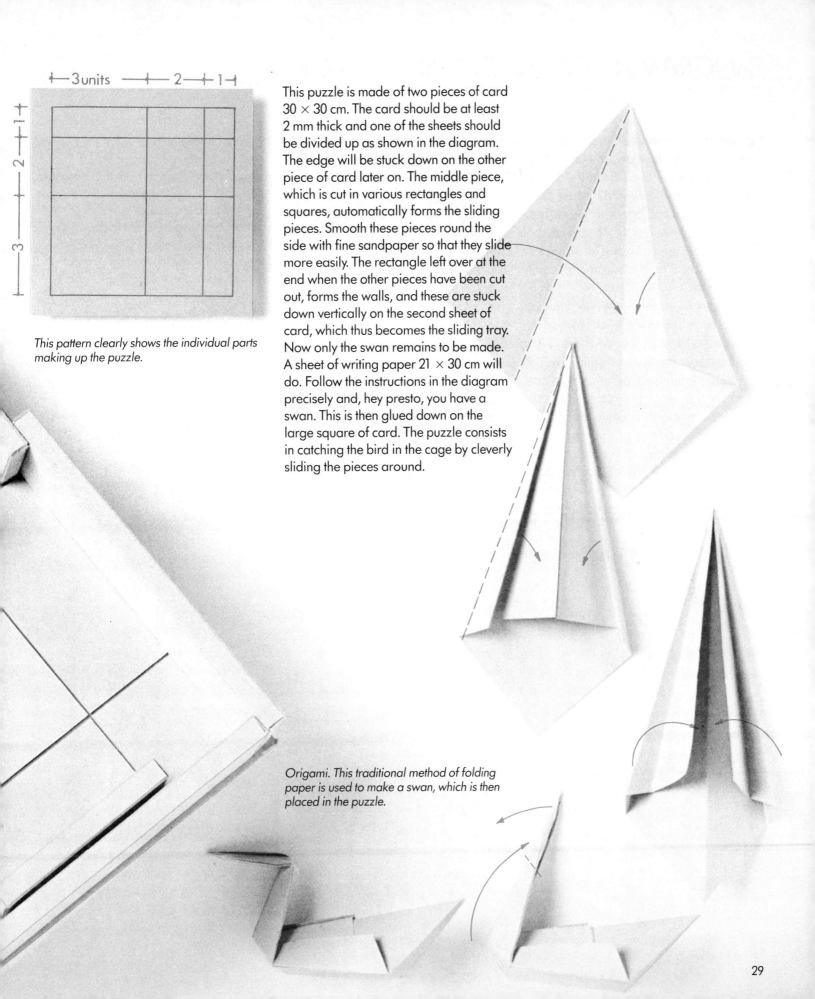

This pattern clearly shows the individual parts making up the puzzle.

This puzzle is made of two pieces of card 30 × 30 cm. The card should be at least 2 mm thick and one of the sheets should be divided up as shown in the diagram. The edge will be stuck down on the other piece of card later on. The middle piece, which is cut in various rectangles and squares, automatically forms the sliding pieces. Smooth these pieces round the side with fine sandpaper so that they slide more easily. The rectangle left over at the end when the other pieces have been cut out, forms the walls, and these are stuck down vertically on the second sheet of card, which thus becomes the sliding tray. Now only the swan remains to be made. A sheet of writing paper 21 × 30 cm will do. Follow the instructions in the diagram precisely and, hey presto, you have a swan. This is then glued down on the large square of card. The puzzle consists in catching the bird in the cage by cleverly sliding the pieces around.

Origami. This traditional method of folding paper is used to make a swan, which is then placed in the puzzle.

TANGRAM: THE PUZZLE AS AN ART FORM

No one knows exactly where Tangram originated. Obviously it was in China, but that is as much as anyone can tell you. The American puzzle expert, Sam Lloyd, seemed to have solved the secret of Tangram many years ago. At any rate he published an entire treatise to show that this game, which had suddenly gained widespread popularity, was actually thought up by the Chinese god, Tan. Lloyd even referred to the seven holy books of Tan, which were purported to contain about ten thousand illustrations of figures which can be made with Tangram. These ten thousand illustrations supposedly represented the story of the Creation.

Later research revealed that Mr. Lloyd must have had a very active imagination. He had even brought in such learned figures as Archimedes and Pythagoras to lend credibility to his theories. Even his so-called 'Tanka girls', who were supposed to have amused sailors with these games in the port of Canton, proved to be figments of his imagination.

Thus Tangram was once again imbued with the spirit of mystery. At the beginning of the nineteenth century the game suddenly became universally popular, and it is even said that Napoleon lightened his last days with the game.

Tangram is a game that consists of seven pieces, made by dividing up a square in a particular way. These parts are put together in such a way that they make all sorts of different figures, the shapes of people and animals, as well as many different artefacts, figures and letters.

Tangram is very easy to make, particularly if you follow the instructions in the diagram very accurately. First, choose the material you are going to use. If this is to be a piece of thick card – suitable for a first attempt – the best size to choose is 10 × 10 cm. On the card draw 16 squares of equal size (see the example), and through these, the thicker lines shown on the diagram. You then cut up the piece of card along the lines shown in the diagram. This inevitably results in one square, a parallelogram (a sort of lopsided square), and five triangles – two large ones, one medium sized one, and two smaller ones. These pieces should be cut out by drawing a sharp knife along a metal ruler. The Tans, the actual pieces of the Tangram, will be nice and sharp if you do this. Obviously the Tans can be decorated in all sorts of ways.

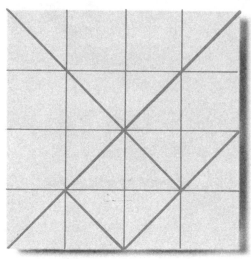

It cannot be denied that Sam Lloyd added a large number of new figures to Tangram. He must have been quite obsessed with the game. For example, he thought up figures representing two different things, depending on the point of view from which they were regarded. A real Tangram enthusiast will always be on the lookout for this sort of figure, but to be honest, it is virtually impossible to come up with any new figures now.

Nevertheless, Tangram is still a game with a remarkable number of possibilities. It's not for nothing that the Chinese call Tangram 'the board of wisdom'. You can make an amazing number of different figures from these seven simple shapes: plump or skinny animals, letters as well as numbers.

Tangram requires a great deal of imagination; and apparently there is even a book on mathematics in which the various geometrical shapes are shown in pieces of Tangram.

Tangram can be viewed as a sort of science, but it can also be considered as an art form. Poets and painters have been inspired by Tangram. They were quite fascinated by this strange game in which pieces which are in themselves so simple and angular are used to make delicate figures. In fact, the pieces themselves can be very artistic. They are sometimes made from beautifully carved wood, or from bone or ivory. In some cases the games are actually extremely valuable works of art.

You can make all sorts of jumping, dancing figures with the seven Tans.

Both these gentlemen are made with seven Tans. But why is it that one has a foot while the other doesn't? They really are the same size.

Try copying these figures. It may prove to be quite difficult, but it's certainly not impossible.

*Try copying these figures. It may prove to be
quite difficult, but it's certainly not impossible.*

Van Deventer thought of this intricate puzzle.
You can spend hours making it.

MATCHBOXES BY VAN DEVENTER

You probably learned your first matchbox trick at a very early age. Slide a full box upside down in the sleeve and it's great fun to watch an unsuspecting member of the family open the box next time. If he opens it with the top facing up – which is more than likely as the force of habit is great – the matches will be scattered all over the floor before he knows where he is!

This is all great fun for a three year old, though no three year old will be able to cope with this advanced matchbox puzzle, thought up quite recently by a young Dutchman, Oskar van Deventer. When Oskar was playing around with some empty matchboxes one day, he developed an extremely sophisticated as well as amusing puzzle, for which he used only five boxes.

With these five boxes he made five models and the game consisted simply of *shutting all the boxes*. This puzzle was published in the Dutch newspaper, the *NRC Handelsblad,* by Leon Vie, who delighted in this fiendishly simple but terrible trick.

All you need are five matchboxes and a tube of good adhesive. The length, width and height measurements should be in the ratio 3:2:1, and the best matchboxes to use are those which measure 4.5 × 3 × 1.5 cm, as these comply with this ratio. Glue the boxes together in the way shown in the illustration.

There are actually three ways of sliding the boxes together, and we will provide the hapless reader with one solution, leaving him to find the other two for himself. Remember that there are also incorrect solutions. It cannot be denied that matchboxes are fairly flexible, and there are those who manage to push the boxes into the sleeves by forcing them – this is a technique which can certainly not be condoned. In other words, any solutions achieved in this way *do not count.*

All you need are 5 matchboxes in order to make this puzzle.

THE PIRATE FLAG

Imagine this. It's 1600, you're sailing off the coast of Dunkirk in an honourable vessel, when suddenly you see a strange galleon draw up alongside. Is it a pirate ship? They're certainly not unknown in these waters. You're ready to give them a broadside when you see that a 'friendly' flag is flying on the mast. It has eight stripes and happens to be that of a friendly nation.

All the orders are cancelled. The cannon are rolled back into place, the sailors start scrubbing the decks, the cook is rattling the pans in the galley when suddenly the flag with the eight stripes changes into a flag with nine stripes. And this is the flag of the infamous pirate, Jean Crévaison. Apparently he had also studied the puzzle with the pirate flag. This puzzle is one in which a 'friendly' flag can change in a fraction of a second into an enemy flag.

The flag with a false bottom.
Follow the diagram exactly when you are making your pirate flag.

You make the pirate flag by drawing a flag with eight stripes on a piece of card 15 × 20 cm about 0.5 mm thick. The example shown here must be followed exactly. Then draw in the stepped diagonal exactly as shown in the example.

Cut out the flag which you have drawn already, with a penknife or scissors, and cut the pirate flag along the stepped diagonals. Then colour the flag any colour you wish and your pirate flag is finished. If you slide the right half down one step and then join the two halves, you will see that the flag which began with eight stripes now has nine stripes. Just what a clever pirate always needed.

41

BRAIN TEASER

It's almost impossible to imagine a more amusing puzzle. These puzzles pose almost insurmountable problems for anyone, and yet in principle even a three year old toddler could solve them. All you need is a flexible mind.

Take this brain teaser, for example. The object is to remove the string from the card without tearing or cutting it. Do you think that it's possible? The French say: *'Simple comme bonjour'*. In other words, 'It's as easy as pie'.

For this puzzle you'll need a piece of flexible card, a length of string and two large beads. If you like, you can also make two small cardboard pyramids to use instead of the beads. Take your pick. Cut two grooves across almost the entire length of the card with a sharp penknife. Then cut a third line at right angles to these grooves and now thread the string through the three cuts.

The puzzle is easy to make. Instead of beads you can use pieces of wood or piramids of cardboard.

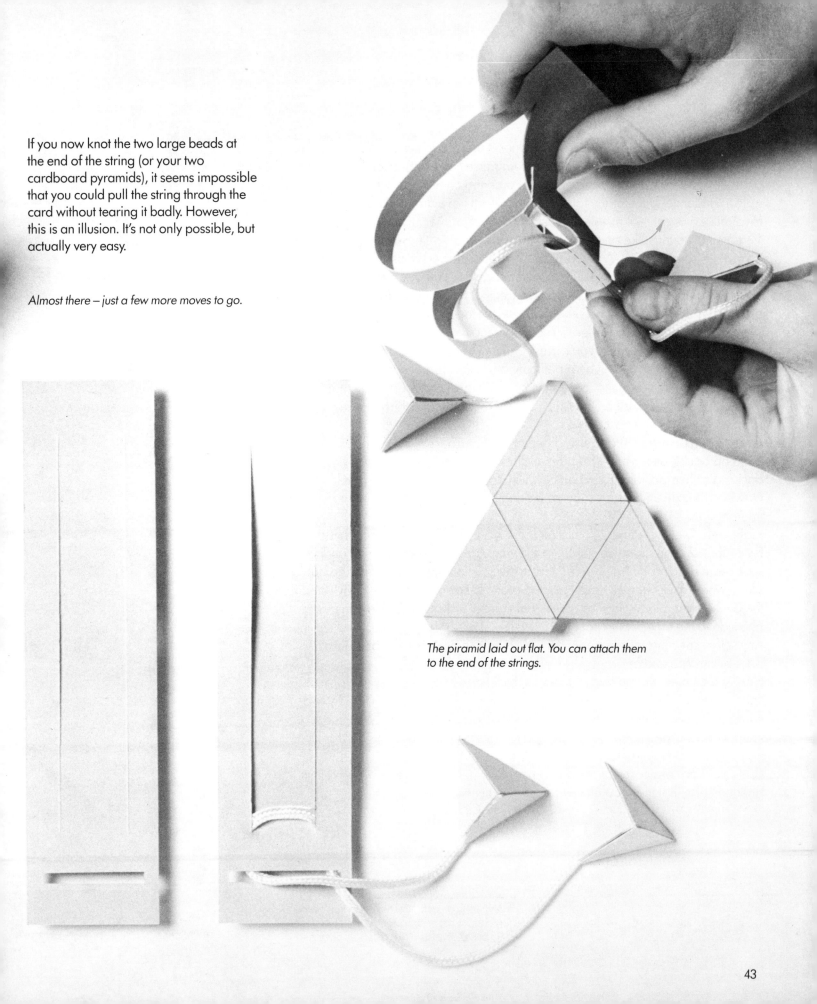

If you now knot the two large beads at the end of the string (or your two cardboard pyramids), it seems impossible that you could pull the string through the card without tearing it badly. However, this is an illusion. It's not only possible, but actually very easy.

Almost there – just a few more moves to go.

The piramid laid out flat. You can attach them to the end of the strings.

PENTOMINOES

This is not a mathematics textbook, nor does it pretend to be one. But in dealing with pentominoes the reader will have to immerse himself in a number of geometrical shapes. If all this is not to become too complicated, he must be able to understand the many false bottoms which have made the pentomino a favourite amongst real puzzle enthusiasts.

'Pentomino' sounds like an advanced move in figure skating, but nothing could be further from the truth. A pentomino, hereafter referred to as a 'pento', is a shape which consists of five squares joined together. Perhaps this seems a rather enigmatic description, but don't forget that two squares joined together are known as a 'domino', the very piece used in the game of dominoes.

When three of these squares are joined together in any shape you like, it's called a tromino, and when you have four squares, it's called a tetromino, so that five joined together will be a pentomino (pento). Just in case you're wondering, there's also a hexomino, consisting of six squares, but this is a bit more than most puzzle enthusiasts can handle. It can be used to make thirty-five different shapes, which is rather excessive.

A pento can be made into twelve different shapes. These twelve shapes – or building bricks, as it were – form respectively the letters I, L, P, T, U, V, W, X ,Y and Z, a rather lopsided F, and an N which doesn't really look like one. However, puzzle enthusiasts may be lacking in many ways, but never in imagination.

Right then. Twelve pentoes. Computer buffs will immediately realize that no fewer than 2339 rectangles can be made with sides of respectively six and ten squares. It should be remembered that in the solution there should not be any place where four pentoes have only one plane in common. Nor is it any good if the pentoes are placed in such a way that there is a straight dividing line from one side to the other of the pattern.

Any self-respecting puzzle freak will be itching to have a go, because the possibilities are endles.

Here we go then. Try making a pattern in the shape of a square with eight small squares on all sides. In the middle you can have a hole measuring two by two squares. It doesn't matter where. You think this is easy, don't you? Well, forget it. There are thousands of possibilities, and it is even more difficult if you want the hole to be in the centre, for there are only fifty-eight solutions.

Pentoes. There are cases on record of people who became so addicted to this phenomenon that they couldn't even stop for dinner.

These are the twelve pentoes. If you look closely, you can actually recognize the letters. However, it's more important to remember that every pento consists of five squares arranged into different patterns.

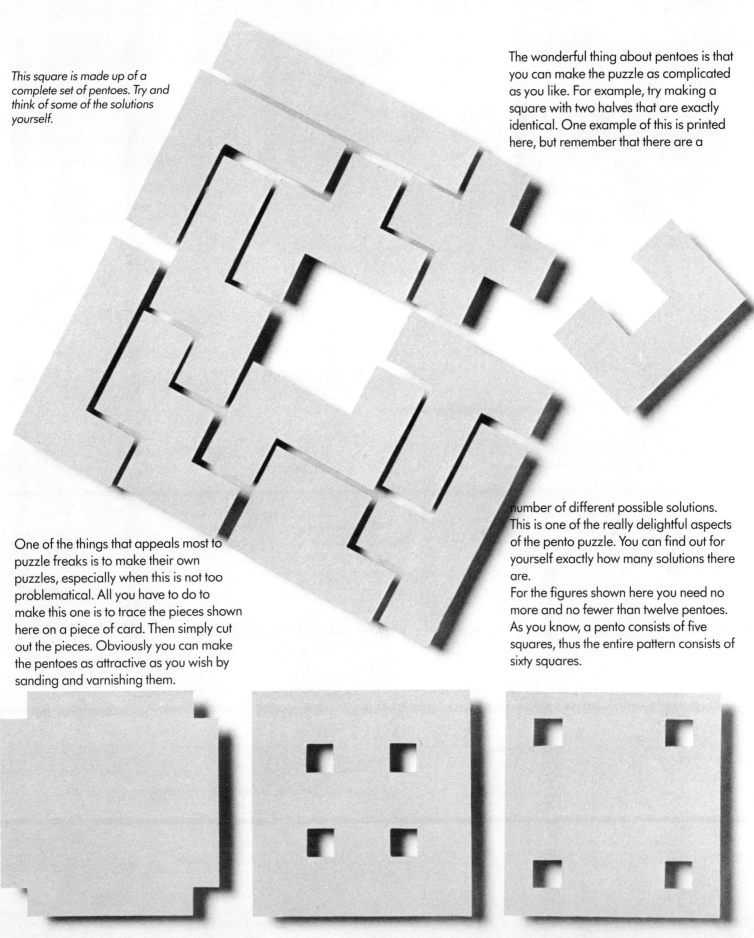

This square is made up of a complete set of pentoes. Try and think of some of the solutions yourself.

The wonderful thing about pentoes is that you can make the puzzle as complicated as you like. For example, try making a square with two halves that are exactly identical. One example of this is printed here, but remember that there are a

One of the things that appeals most to puzzle freaks is to make their own puzzles, especially when this is not too problematical. All you have to do to make this one is to trace the pieces shown here on a piece of card. Then simply cut out the pieces. Obviously you can make the pentoes as attractive as you wish by sanding and varnishing them.

number of different possible solutions. This is one of the really delightful aspects of the pento puzzle. You can find out for yourself exactly how many solutions there are.

For the figures shown here you need no more and no fewer than twelve pentoes. As you know, a pento consists of five squares, thus the entire pattern consists of sixty squares.

All the patterns shown here can be made with pentoes. Obviously the pentoes must not overlap. Don't stop when you've found one solution because there are always other solutions possible.

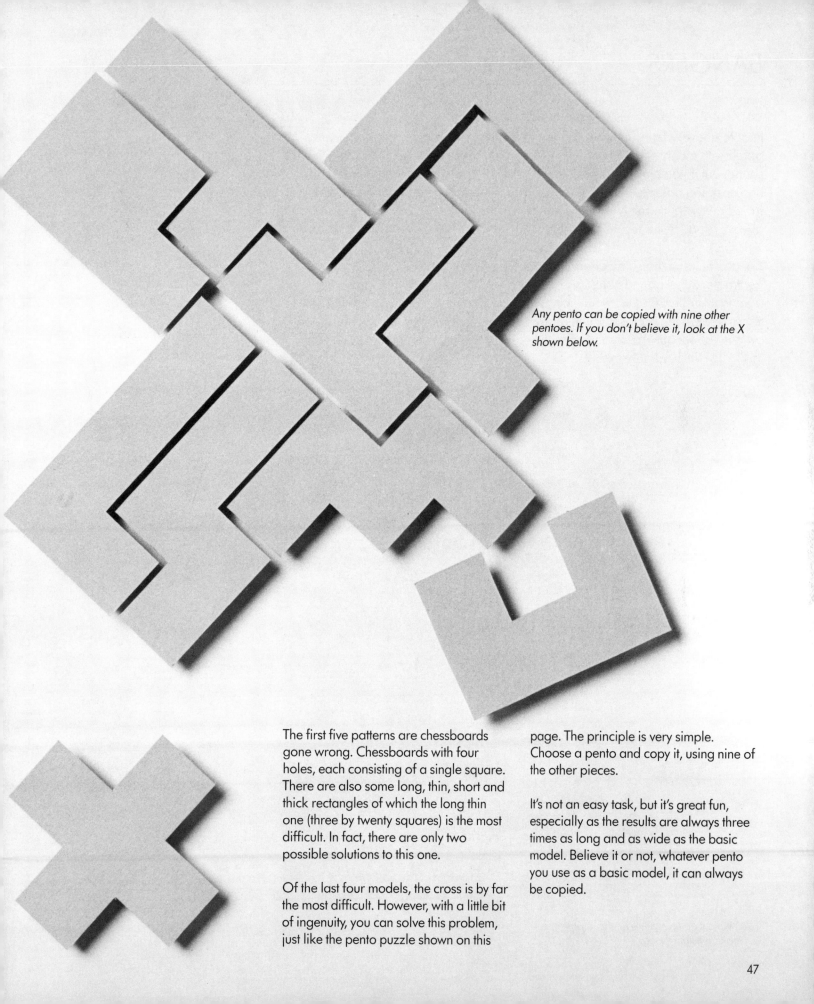

Any pento can be copied with nine other pentoes. If you don't believe it, look at the X shown below.

The first five patterns are chessboards gone wrong. Chessboards with four holes, each consisting of a single square. There are also some long, thin, short and thick rectangles of which the long thin one (three by twenty squares) is the most difficult. In fact, there are only two possible solutions to this one.

Of the last four models, the cross is by far the most difficult. However, with a little bit of ingenuity, you can solve this problem, just like the pento puzzle shown on this page. The principle is very simple. Choose a pento and copy it, using nine of the other pieces.

It's not an easy task, but it's great fun, especially as the results are always three times as long and as wide as the basic model. Believe it or not, whatever pento you use as a basic model, it can always be copied.

BANGERS

People are very funny creatures. If you're beating a carpet in your own front porch with a carpet beater, no one will give it a second thought. It's a familiar sound. But if you blow up a paper bag to bursting point and then punch it hard, unsuspecting passers-by will be cringing even before the echo of the bang has faded away. It's certainly a very old trick, but the joker with a paper bag can always produce the results he wants.

You can achieve the same effect with a piece of paper, and especially with a banknote, a five pound note, for example. Hold the sharp edge of the note against your lips, and blow while you make a tearing movement with one hand, sharp against the edge. This will really annoy your companions, but they'll be even more put out when you suddenly make the note bang. You really can do this — look at the diagram.

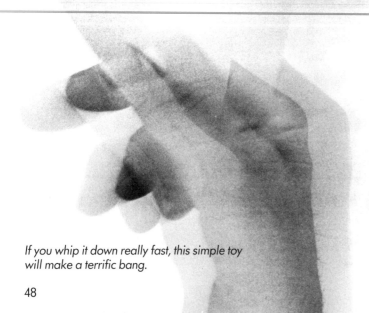

If you whip it down really fast, this simple toy will make a terrific bang.

Follow the instructions step by step to fold your banger.

All you need for this trifling sound production is a sheet of paper, e.g., from a writing pad. You fold this as shown in the example, to make a triangle. Hold the triangle between the thumb and index finger at the bottom, and with a quick flick of the wrist, whip it down. If you do it properly, you'll find this makes a loud bang.

If it doesn't work, try again with thicker paper, though it's also possible that you didn't 'whip' the triangle down correctly. This takes a little practice. In fact, the better you execute the whip, and the thicker the card, the louder the bang will be.

THE MAGIC PURSE

Perhaps you were once given a box of conjuring tricks for your birthday when you were little. It certainly must have contained a Magic Purse. Real magic. You could amaze your audience without doing anything really clever. The Magic Purse did the trick all by itself.

You'd get someone to put a pound note, a fiver or even more into the Magic Purse, and just for effect, you'd mutter the magic words, and hey presto: the note would have moved in the depths of the magic purse from one side to the other, and was now held on the left, behind a few strips.
This was by no means the end of the trick. When the purse was closed again, another spell was muttered, the purse would open again... and this time the note would appear on the other side of the purse, to everyone's great surprise. How was this possible and how did it work?

The trick was in the purse of course. It's very easy to make this purse yourself. You don't need to dig out your old box of conjuring tricks – it takes no longer to make your own magic purse than it does to search the attic looking for the one you used to have. In fact, it's child's play.

The Magic Purse makes a good present. Follow the diagram carefully when you make your own Magic Purse.

more, and – well, well – you've done it again – the paper's on the other side. You're a real conjuror.

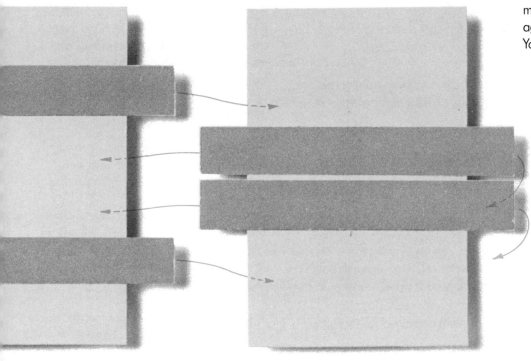

Take two pieces of card 8 × 15 cm long and 1 cm wide. Place the strips between the pieces of card at equal distances. The ends of the strips should stick out beyond the cards. Now fold the strips over the pieces of card in such a way that the two middle strips can be stuck down at the top and the two outer strips are stuck down at the bottom.

That's all there is to it. If you've got it right, the strips are attached to both the right and left side of the purse, and the purse can be folded open in two directions. Obviously it's a good idea to check that the magic works with a piece of paper first. Put this in the purse, shut it, open it out again and you'll see that the paper seems to be held between the two strips. Now shut the purse again – open it once

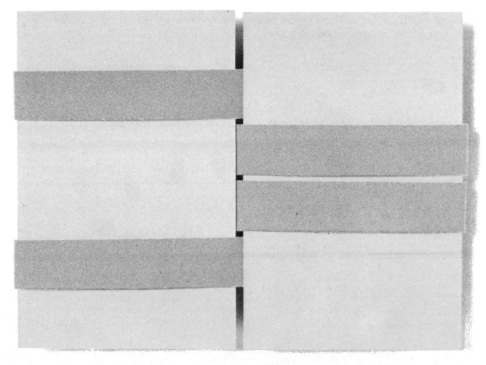

GAMBLING 1

Apparently drinking, smoking and gambling don't do a person any good, or so it's said. Yet whatever they might say, gambling of the sort described here can't do any harm. At worst you might give up on it, but then it is a puzzle.

What's it all about? These four special dice don't have six faces numbered one to six (like normal dice). Instead, these dice only have faces numbered one, two, three and four.

Obviously this is for a reason, and in fact, the reason can be explained as follows. Put the dice together in a row so that all four numbers are visible on every side of the row. An innocent reader might make the mistake of thinking that at last there's going to be an easy puzzle, but he'd be very wrong. The chance of finding the solution just by trying your luck is 1:40,000.

According to Trevor Rice, who published this problem in his book *Mathematical Games and Puzzles,* a number of variations on this puzzle have come onto the market. They've even appeared in soap advertisements and on flags and symbols on maps. The dice have also been made with coloured faces rather than numbers.

This particular dice variation has never been published or made before. So if you solve it, you may be the first person in the world to do so. That's a rather neat idea.

For these extra special dice you need a piece of card 17 × 13 cm, about 0.5 mm thick. If you're rather parsimonious by nature, slide the models together when you're cutting them out. In this case you'll need a piece of card 40 × 50 cm for the four dice.

Follow the diagram carefully when you trace it and cut out the card, and then draw in the dots on the faces of the dice while it is still folded open.
Follow the example exactly or you'll find yourself in dire trouble. In fact, the puzzle may even be insoluble. Score along the lines with a penknife, and then glue the dice.

Tip: the way in which we have placed the dice may actually help you find the solution, though you'll still find it quite a puzzle to do. Another idea is to make a note of the number of solutions you find, and try to organise a competition with your friends.

At first glance you might not think so, but these extra special dice conceal an enormous problem.

52

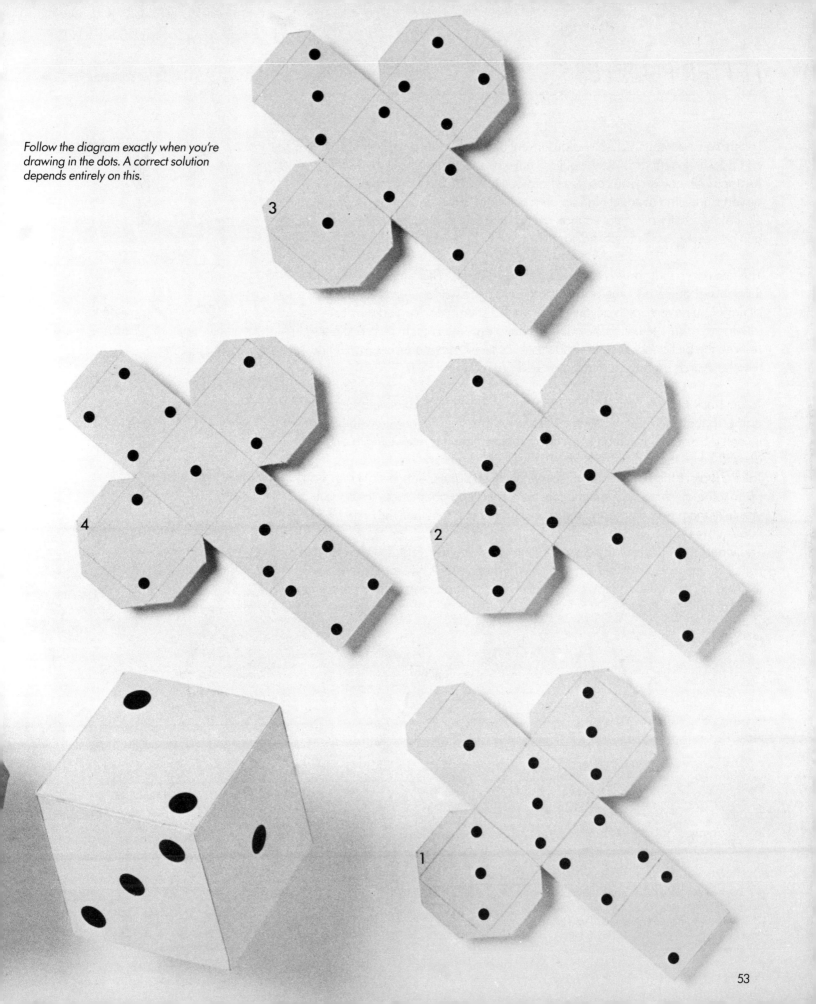

Follow the diagram exactly when you're drawing in the dots. A correct solution depends entirely on this.

LETTER PUZZLES

Letters were obviously a marvellous invention. There are so many things you can do with letters. This book couldn't have been made without them, for example. Of course, you can use enormous letters to spell out a message advertising some product high up on a building. In the UK, letters are made of chocolate, pastry or pasta, so that you can eat your own initials. Finally, letters can be used to make fantastic puzzles.

The first game that springs to mind must be Scrabble. This simple but cleverly thought out game became popular throughout the world in a very short space of time. You haven't seen anything until you've seen a doctor and a priest playing Scrabble in Latin. They don't seem to agree on much and constantly refer to the dictionary to settle disputes. In case you're wondering, you'll find that the church usually triumphs over science in the end.

To get back to letter puzzles. A certain Harvey Lindgren also developed a game, though Lindgren was never as successful as his colleague who had invented Scrabble (this man soon became a millionaire). However, this certainly doesn't mean that the game is worthless. On the contrary.
Take a look at the block capitals shown on these pages. At first sight they don't seem to be anything very special, but the nicest thing about these letters is that if you take the pieces apart and then move them back together, they can be made into squares.
The V and Y are particularly difficult to make, while the X and Z, which look rather daunting at first sight, are actually fairly simple. A hint for those who are inclined to give up straightaway: sometimes it's a good idea to turn the asymmetrical pieces around.

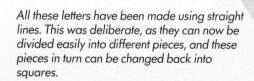

All these letters have been made using straight lines. This was deliberate, as they can now be divided easily into different pieces, and these pieces in turn can be changed back into squares.

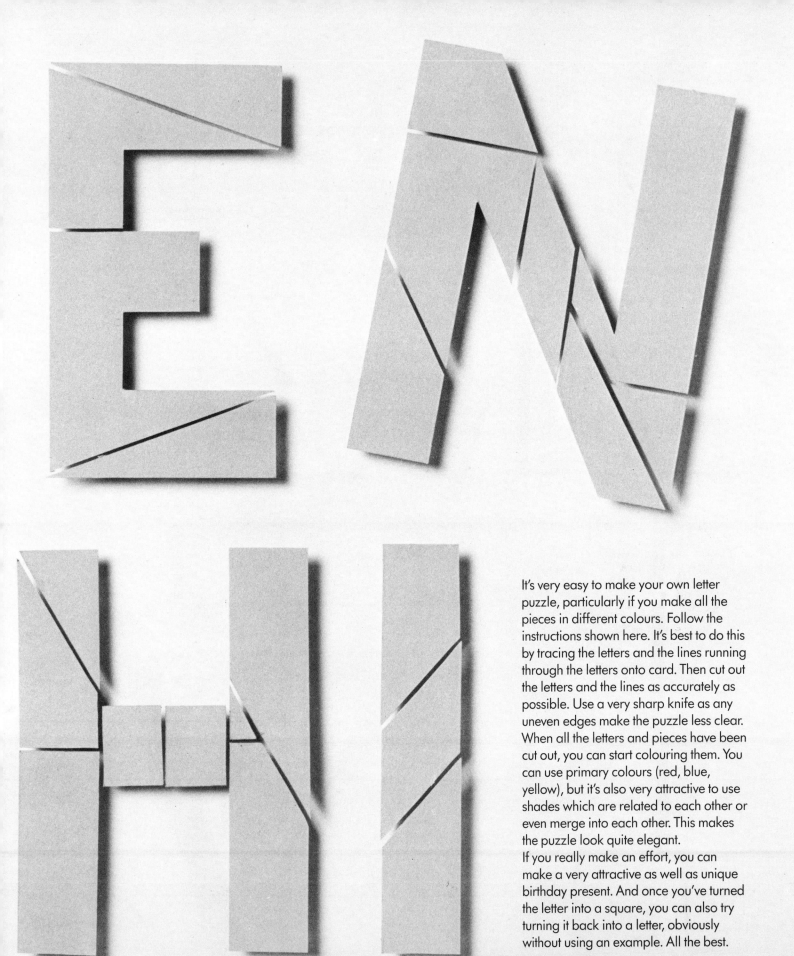

It's very easy to make your own letter puzzle, particularly if you make all the pieces in different colours. Follow the instructions shown here. It's best to do this by tracing the letters and the lines running through the letters onto card. Then cut out the letters and the lines as accurately as possible. Use a very sharp knife as any uneven edges make the puzzle less clear. When all the letters and pieces have been cut out, you can start colouring them. You can use primary colours (red, blue, yellow), but it's also very attractive to use shades which are related to each other or even merge into each other. This makes the puzzle look quite elegant.

If you really make an effort, you can make a very attractive as well as unique birthday present. And once you've turned the letter into a square, you can also try turning it back into a letter, obviously without using an example. All the best.

F

This is how you make squares from the divided letters.

THE SILHOUETTOSCOPE

Apperently there was once a French minister of finance called de Silhouette. This man's hobby was to outline people's faces on paper and then fill in the outlines in black. The trick has continued to be popular over the centuries and this sort of drawing is now known by the name of the minister: silhouette.

These silhouettes serve as a basis for the Silhouettoscope, which is rather a fancy name for a priceless and very unusual puzzle. Moreover, it's fairly easy to construct, which makes the Silhouettoscope an extremely suitable present for your friends. You could also call it 'Find the rabbit', as it all started with this cleverly concealed rodent inside the Silhouettoscope.

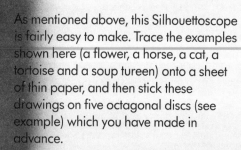

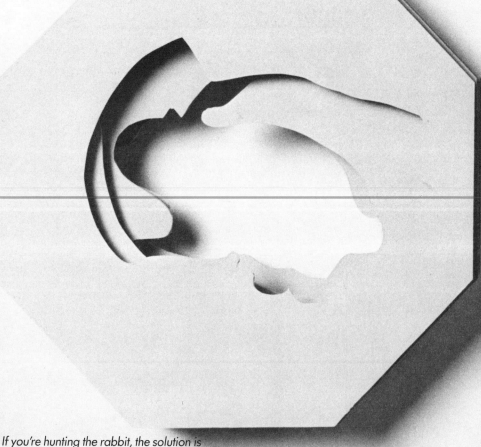

If you're hunting the rabbit, the solution is shown above.

As mentioned above, this Silhouettoscope is fairly easy to make. Trace the examples shown here (a flower, a horse, a cat, a tortoise and a soup tureen) onto a sheet of thin paper, and then stick these drawings on five octagonal discs (see example) which you have made in advance.

Use a very sharp knife to cut the pictures from the discs, and place these discs one on top of the other. Sooner or later you'll see a rabbit appearing. If you want to make the Silhouettoscope even more special, you can varnish the discs or cover them with Fablon, a sticky-backed coloured plastic covering you can buy in decorators' shops.

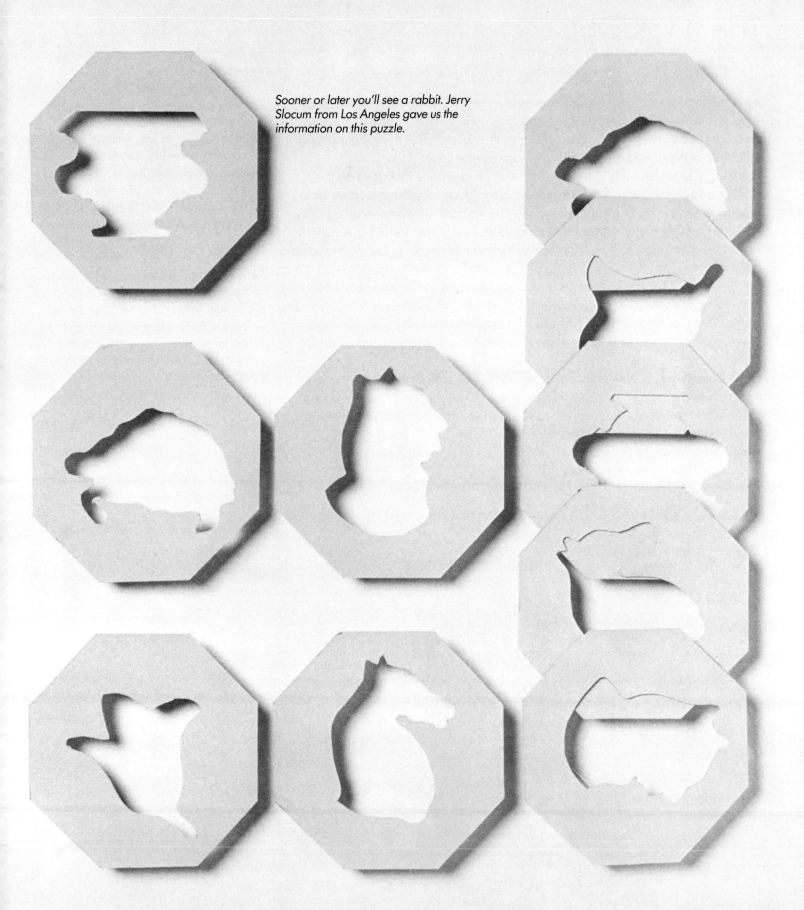

Sooner or later you'll see a rabbit. Jerry Slocum from Los Angeles gave us the information on this puzzle.

THE MAGIC DISC

It's a striking fact that the simplest games are often considered to be the most fun. It's an all too familiar sight to see an expensive birthday gift, like a brand new bright red fire engine with searchlights that work, left in the toy cupboard in favour of building a fort made out of logs for the fire.

The Magic Disc definitely comes under the latter category. It's based on the well-known buzzer, one of the large buttons threaded with string that we all played with once upon a time. After a few preliminary twirls, you had to pull as hard as possible on the ends of the string so that the button would spin faster and faster and begin to hum. Finally the string would break or become tangled up in your fingers.

For the Magic Disc the button has been replaced by a cardboard disc that you can make yourself. (NB For a picture of the well-known buzzer, see the opposite page.) This disc is fixed to the string, not horizontally but vertically. In this way you can make use of both sides of the disc and this is precisely what it's all about.

If you draw two complementary pictures on the two sides, you can achieve a very amusing effect. The picture on one side isn't very clear, the picture on the other side is rather abstract, but when you start spinning the disc on the string, you'll suddenly see a particular picture.

Two 'Japanese characters' can turn into the face of Donald Duck. In fact, with the Magic Disc, anything is possible.

The Magic Disc is easy to make, even for someone with two left hands! Cut out the disc with a knife or with scissors from a piece of card about 1 mm thick. It should have a diameter of 7-8 cm and you need four holes in the disc in the place shown on the diagram. These are the holes for the string, which should be about 120 cm long.

Glue two small pieces of lead (or wire) on the top and bottom edge with superglue. Then draw your illustrations on each side. Remember that the picture on the back should be upside down. If you want to use the illustrations from this book, trace them onto a thin sheet of paper and stick them down on the card.

These two 'abstract' drawings make a clear picture when the disc is humming.

The old-fashioned buzzer made with one of grandpa's trouser buttons.

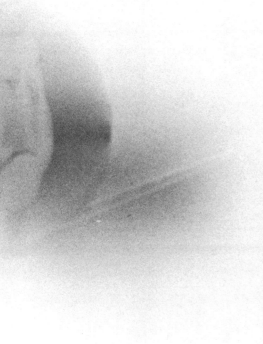

The front and back of the Magic Disc weighted with a little piece of lead and with a drawing on either side.

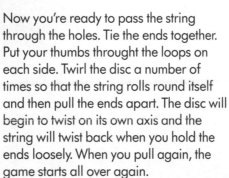

Now you're ready to pass the string through the holes. Tie the ends together. Put your thumbs throught the loops on each side. Twirl the disc a number of times so that the string rolls round itself and then pull the ends apart. The disc will begin to twist on its own axis and the string will twist back when you hold the ends loosely. When you pull again, the game starts all over again.

This is high level magic. You make the hole simply by turning the card over.

INTO THIN AIR

Wouldn't it be wonderful to do real magic, to be a magician. There are people like this. They can show us things that aren't there – or are they?

You can be sure of everyone's interest if you can change a red tomato into a white one with blue spots, or a cup of coffee into a glass of beer with a head of foam. Even the man who can conjure up a dove from his top hat is a magician, and so is the sinister gentleman with the evil grin on his hideous face who goes around sawing beautiful girls in half.

And yet, you know all the time that you're being taken for a ride. In fact, you're just being had. All the same, isn't it fun to pull someone's leg? Try it yourself with this card. It starts off with a hole in it that later disappears.

Do you think it's difficult to make? Not at all. Or difficult to do? Certainly not. Do you think it'll work? Without a doubt. It may be very simple but it's also amazingly convincing. Five seconds ago you were convinced that there was a perfectly square hole in the card, then suddenly there's nothing. The eye can't follow this, and certainly the mind can't, except the mind of the magician himself.

This magic card is very easy to make. Take a piece of card 14 × 22.8 cm and find a sharp Stanley knife and an absolutely straight ruler. Then copy the lines from the model shown here, but make sure that you do so precisely, as complete accuracy is of the utmost importance.

Now cut the card into pieces along the lines and you'll see that there's no hole in the magic card. However, when you turn it over and slide the pieces together, you'll see a hole in it.

All this is as easy as pie, but if you want to be absolutely certain of success, decorate the card as a playing card. This is particularly effective if you make, for example, the Queen of Hearts so that the face of the Queen appears exactly in the hole. Or you could also do the King of Hearts.

Copy the model accurately onto a piece of card... and cut the whole thing out with a Stanley knife.

THE STARS SHINE EVERYWHERE

You can make the most fantastic constructions out of paper. This is a well-known fact. What's not so well-known is that these constructions are much easier to make than you'd think at first sight. Even if you've never heard of the Ancient Greek surveyvor, Pythagoras, you'll still be quite capable of folding one of these mathematical figures. All you need is some dexterity and perseverance.

Obviously you'll also need the materials. In the first place, there should be a few sheets of thick paper (preferably in various colours), and in addition, you'll need a large tube of adhesive, a ruler and a sharp Stanley knife. You can also use the ruler in combination with a set square.

If you wish to make one of the shapes described on this page and the following pages, it's best to trace the templates onto thin or transparent paper. (The templates are the folded pieces of paper or card used to make the shape.) When you've traced the lines onto paper, transfer them onto the coloured paper or card with a sheet of tracing paper.

If you think that the stars shown in this book are too small, you can make larger ones. The sizes of the examples will have to be multiplied by the factor you choose. For larger stars, use thicker card otherwise the models will be very floppy. You'll need to score along the fold lines with a Stanley knife if you're using thicker card in order to get the sharp edges along the fold. These stars are obviously very suitable for hanging on the Christmas tree or simply to put on your bookcase. If you decide to paint them after you've constructed them, take into account the type of paper you have used. Some paper will go very soggy when it is painted with watercolours. It's much better to use acrylic paints.

STAR 1

The first of this series of stars is actually a very simple star. Appearances are deceptive and this star is no exception. In theory it consists of two tetrahedra – these are explained earlier in the book – but in practice it consists of one large tetrahedron and four small pyramids. These four pyramids are stuck against the sides of the tetrahedron.

NB The shapes below have to be copied four times before you can make this star and place it on your bedside table as your first trophy. Remember to score along the fold lines so that you can make sharper folds for a more beautiful star.

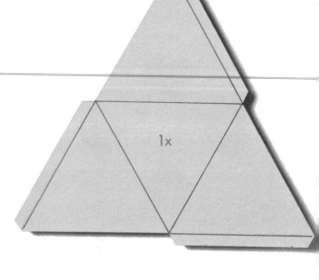

Follow the shape of this example accurately when you are copying and cutting it.

*This easy but beautiful star can be made very
quickly from a few pieces of card.*

Without realizing it, you turn into a mathematician when you're making this star.

STAR 2

This star can be made in two ways. This doesn't mean that you should choose the easier way – it may not be of the highest quality. However, the easier star is described first so as not to frighten you off the more difficult version. (But what is difficult?)

We begin by making 12 models shaped like pentagons. Score the lines and glue the pieces together so that this forms the star, which is known as a dodecahedron. Then make 12 shapes for the 12 pyramids, which are also scored and folded, and then stuck down on the 12 planes of the dodecahedron.

It's more difficult to use the method in which the star is made up of 12 five-pointed stars, as demonstrated on this page. The points are cut out at the base with a cut the depth of the thickness of the card.

It's very important that they are assembled in the right order. Start by forming one point and then start forming the points round this point in a circle, so that you automatically arrive opposite the point where you started.

This star can be made in two ways using these templates.

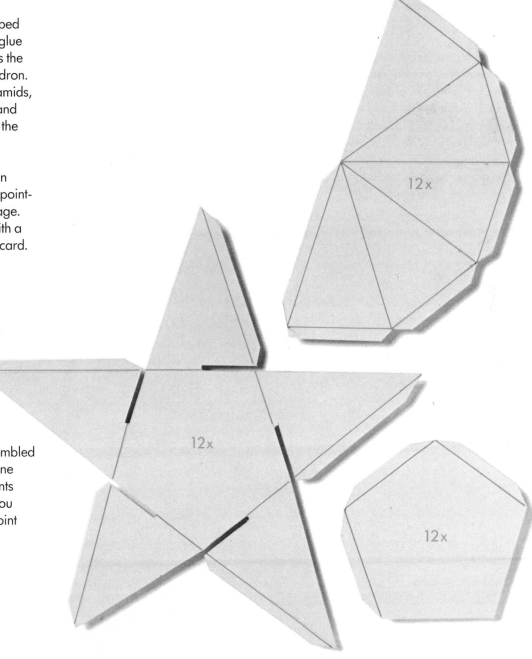

12x

12x

12x

STAR 3

It may be rather an exaggeration to claim that this is the star of all stars, but there's no doubt that this version is very impressive, particularly when you make a large one. However, be warned, it's not an easy star to make. Take your time to choose what method you wish to use to make it, as there are a number of different ways of doing it.

We believe that the best results are obtained with 60 diamond-shaped pieces of card, exactly the size given in the example. The diamonds should be scored through the middle and folded, as should the glue flaps on the side. Start assembling the star at an arbitrary point and don't be discouraged by the fact that eventually it'll have 20 points.

You can also make this star with 20 models (see example) which each form a complete point when they have been folded and glued. Stick these bases against one another with sellotape in the centre of the star so that it cannot be seen. Obviously you cannot do this with

the last point. To stick this one down you need to be quite dexterous and ingenious, as well as the possessor of a tube of adhesive.

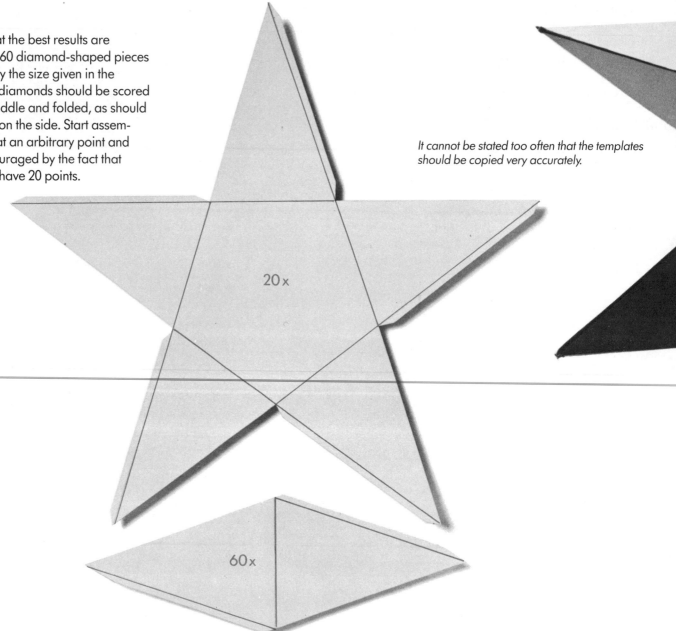

It cannot be stated too often that the templates should be copied very accurately.

20 x

60 x

A few of these stars in your room will furnish it.

This shape looks complicated but it's comparatively easy to make.

STAR 4

This is such a beautiful star that it almost hurts to look at it. However, as the enthusiastic reader probably suspects, it's not particularly easy to make. Nevertheless, we advise you to have a go, as your sense of satisfaction will be even greater when it's finished.

You'll need 20 templates for this many-pointed star and woe betide you if you're even half a millimetre out from the example shown here. Score and fold the templates as shown in the diagram, and stick together each of the 20 elements individually. Then join these 20 elements together to form the work of art illustrated. It's best to use sellotape to stick the points together. The last point fits on rather like a lid, so use a tube of adhesive – but it's still a rather fiddly job. Even so, this beautiful star was probably easier to make than you thought. And so you see, you should never be discouraged before you start.

This template must be traced and drawn very accurately to obtain the results shown here.

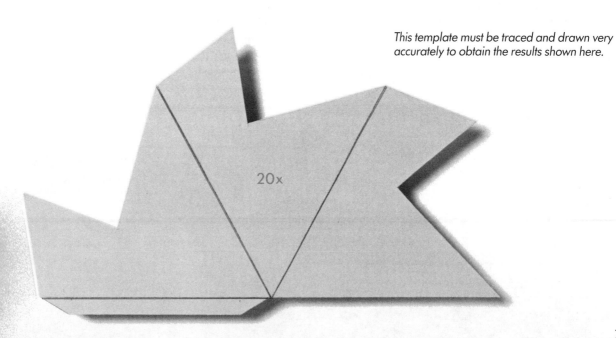

20x

STAR 5

Stars not only come in all sorts of sizes but also in all sorts of shapes. This is rather a special one. You could call it a blunted or circular star. Whatever you call it, it's certainly beautiful and it's not really difficult to make. Certainly the template is very simple.

You will need 20 of these templates. Score along the lines and form into pyramids. Then use the flap to glue them together. You'll need sellotape to join all the elements to the base until you come to the last point. To stick this you will have to fiddle about with a tube of adhesive.

It's quite interesting to stick down only one side of the last point. In this way you can not only show anyone who's interested the inside of this star, but it also means that you could use the star as a lamp if you wished. In this case you leave the point open to change the bulb when necessary. Obviously you would have to make the star of a transparent material in this case, and as small lamps are not very useful, it's a good idea to make the star fairly large. If you do want to make a lamp, you must make sure that the bulb doesn't touch the inside and that the lamp is big enough so that it doesn't get hot. Use a low-wattage bulb.

A simple template. But you'll need twenty before you can assemble the whole star.

20x

This is a star with endless possibilities. You can also use it to make a letter box. But this is a devilishly difficult puzzle. To do this, cut the star open with a Stanley knife after you have first assembled it. If you do it properly the whole star forms a template. It's a fairly difficult problem but we'll give you a clue. Ever heard of symmetry? Of course you have, and that's the clue.

Once you've put together this 'round' star, it's really interesting to cut it apart again.

A star like a cathedral. It will look very decorative hanging from the ceiling, or on the Christmas tree, painted in different bright colours.

STAR 6

This is a magnificent star like a cathedral. If you attempt this one, be warned. To be specific, it's an enormous job, a real challenge, but really worth it when you've finished.

This star should be made from hexagonal pyramids, also known as cosahedra. There's no need to remember the name – the rest is difficult enough as it is. You'll need twenty copies of these six-sided pyramids, so start by scoring along the lines, folding and then gluing them together. Then they need to be assembled. As for all the other stars in this section, remember that it's important to be very accurate regarding the sizes shown in the diagram. There should be no gaps or holes in any star, least of all, this one.

Obviously you will have to join the twenty pyramids together with sellotape to complete the star. Instead of sellotape you can also use pieces of card glued in advance. It's not quite as easy, but the star will be stronger.

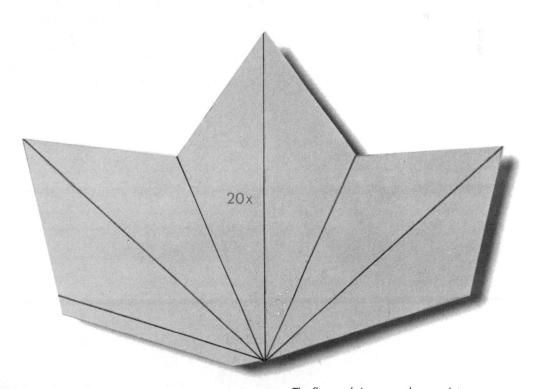

20x

The flap ends in a very sharp point.

A star with a diameter of one metre. Your friends will be quite envious. If you're not careful, you'll literally poke their eyes out.

STAR 7

This twelve-pointed star is long and slender and particularly elegant. For an unknown reason this is the star that is found all over the place at Christmas time. You'll see it hanging in people's windows, often with a ligth inside it. But the same star could also be used as a lantern in the garden in summer, or in the autumn in your room. There's no reason why you shouldn't make quite a few, they're so beautiful.

This star consists of pentagonal points made from the template shown in the example on this page. If you want to make a really impressive star, spend a few pennies and make one with a diameter of one metre or thereabouts. This requires quite a pile of card, but then the results will be really worthwhile.

Naturally the usual rules that apply to making small stars are even more important for making the larger stars. When you're measuring and drawing the lines you should work extremely accurately or you'll end up with a star you can see right through. This is certainly not what you want. Remember to score along the lines carefully, especially towards the points. This is absolutely essential for the star to have perfectly sharp points.

As usual, it's rather a fiddly job to join the last point of the star, as it's difficult to get at the base. However, it is actually possible – so don't give up.

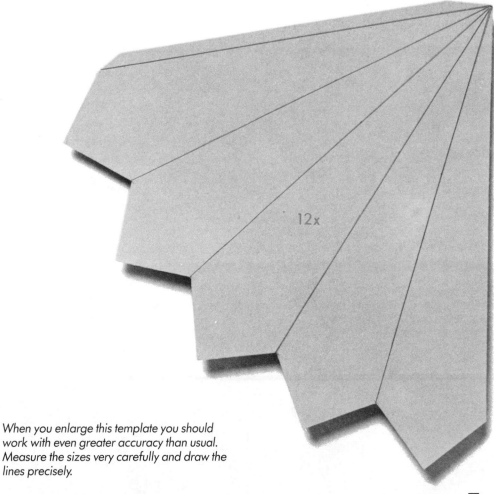

12x

When you enlarge this template you should work with even greater accuracy than usual. Measure the sizes very carefully and draw the lines precisely.

STAR 8

This star is a real sensation. You won't believe your eyes. Of course, it was bound to happen sooner or later. We have described a large number of stars in which all of the points are the same length, but this time the star has points of different lengths. Obviously this means that it's difficult to make, and it's not that easy to cut out or stick together either.

Nevertheless, this star is well worth making. Imagine it covered in glitter. Believe it or not, looking like this it can evoke the Christmas spirit in the middle of July. This is good fun when you come back from a day on the beach.

This is a complicated star, but it's worth summoning up the necessary patience to cut out the 12 + 20 templates (32 in all) very carefully and accurately. You'll surprise even yourself with the results of all your efforts.

Because of its complicated shape, it's difficult to join the points of the star together in the usual way with a little flap for the glue. This time you could use magic tape, ie, invisible tape. However, for those who want to use the small glued flaps, an example is included.

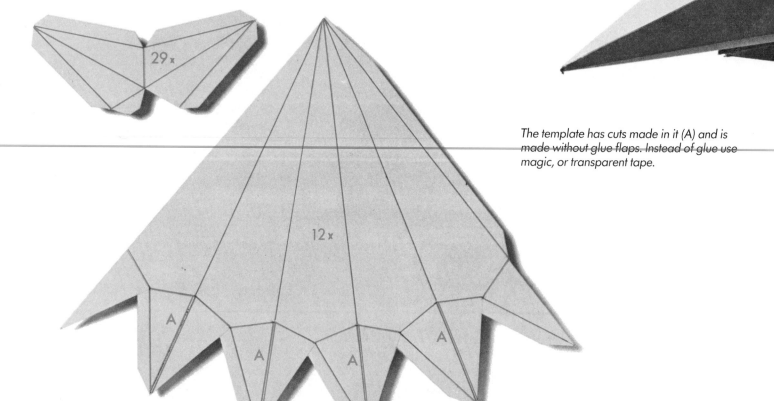

The template has cuts made in it (A) and is made without glue flaps. Instead of glue use magic, or transparent tape.

When you begin making this star, you're embarking on a great adventure. But perhaps the challenge of science is inspiring you to make it.

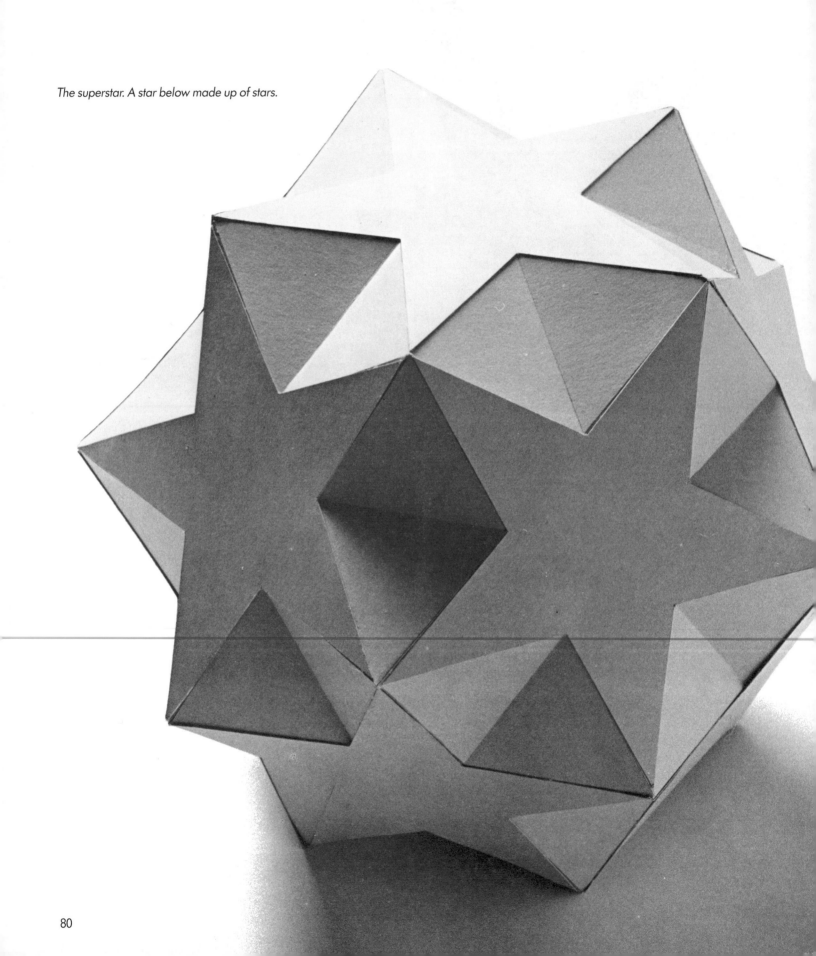

The superstar. A star below made up of stars.

STAR 9

Sound the trumpets and let the drums roll. This star is composed of other stars – in other words, a superstar. It is kept together by 28 diamonds folded into two triangles, each with flaps for gluing which keep the whole thing together.

For this model you can use a slightly thicker type of card. As you can see in the picture, the corners do not have to be folded particularly sharply.

This star should be made exactly according to the example without deviating from it at all.

You can do all sorts of things with this splendid star. Hang it by a thread from the ceiling. You could make a few of them and hang them at different levels. You could stick stickers or silver foil on them or simply make them with coloured paper. A birthday present will look very attractive if it is wrapped up in one of these stars, and it also means that you don't have to give such an expensive present as the star surrounding it is already a generous gesture. Lastly, you can put the star down anywhere as an ornament – on the table, the mantlepiece or wherever.

Twelve of the stars and twenty-eight of these diamonds are needed to make the superstar.

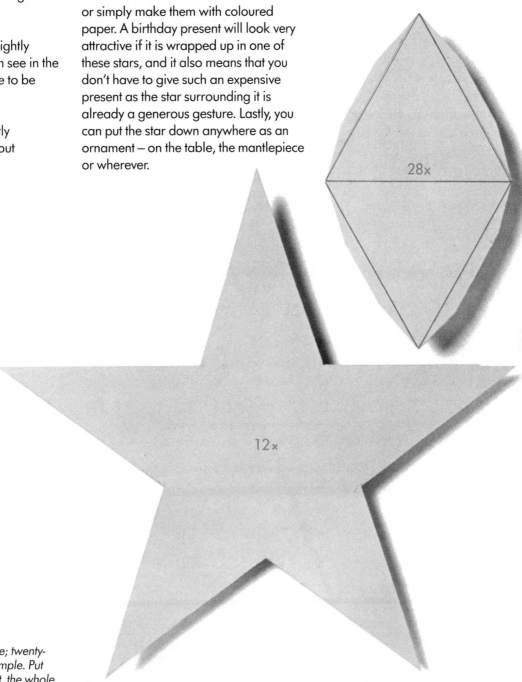

28x

12x

Twelve stars following the example; twenty-eight diamonds following the example. Put them all together as shown. In fact, the whole process is self-evident.

NOW YOU SEE IT, NOW YOU DON'T

This trick has been around for a hundred years, and yet you won't believe your eyes. Anyone with a bit of sense wil realise there's something wrong. But the question remains, what exactly is wrong?

It's certainly strange that a piece of card on which you've drawn eight times eight squares can throw overboard one of these squares simply by sliding it about. There were 64 squares and now there are only 63. How on earth is this possible?

To make it even better, you can make a few more simple manoeuvres so that the square sheet becomes rectangular and suddenly there are 65 squares. How can this be? You started off with 64 squares (admittedly you drew them yourself, but just to make sure, you counted them again), then there were 63, and now there are 65.

Obviously there's an explanation for all this. One was given in 1858, but why should we publish it here for you straightaway? Start by making the model shown here and try and solve the enigma. If you still don't understand, read on, for it's no good showing other people a trick to which you don't know the answer yourself.

As usual, the puzzle is much easier to make than to solve. You need a thick piece of card 16 × 16 cm and between 0.5 and 1 mm thick. Divide the sheet into exactly 8 × 8 squares so that each square is 2 × 2 cm.

Then you emphasize the line that runs horizontally below the third square from the top, and you draw a thick line from the top left corner to the bottom right corner of the square furthest to the right and third from the top (ie, where the thick horizontal line touches the right side), and from the bottom left corner of the bottom square fourth from the left to the top right corner of the third square from the right, fourth from the top.

If this all sounds rather complicated, see the diagram. This should be much easier to understand.

Right. Now cut out the four pieces along the thick lines with a Stanley knife and start sliding.

Tip. It's much easier to slide the pieces when you round off the sharp edges with a blunt object. In addition, you can turn the card into a really attractive piece by colouring it or covering it with glitter. In these cases a little imagination goes a long way.

Finally, we were going to explain to the uncomprehending reader how the squares could mysteriously appear and disappear. Place the four cards in the pattern of the rectangle. Do you notice anything about the diagonal? If you look closely, you'll see that the diagonal does not join. The gap which results is exactly the area of one square. Try and find out for yourself how this square has disappeared again in the other configuration.

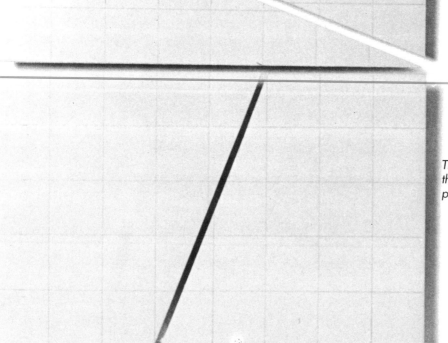

These pieces of card were cut in this way for the first time at least a century ago. It's an old puzzle, but no less exciting for all that.

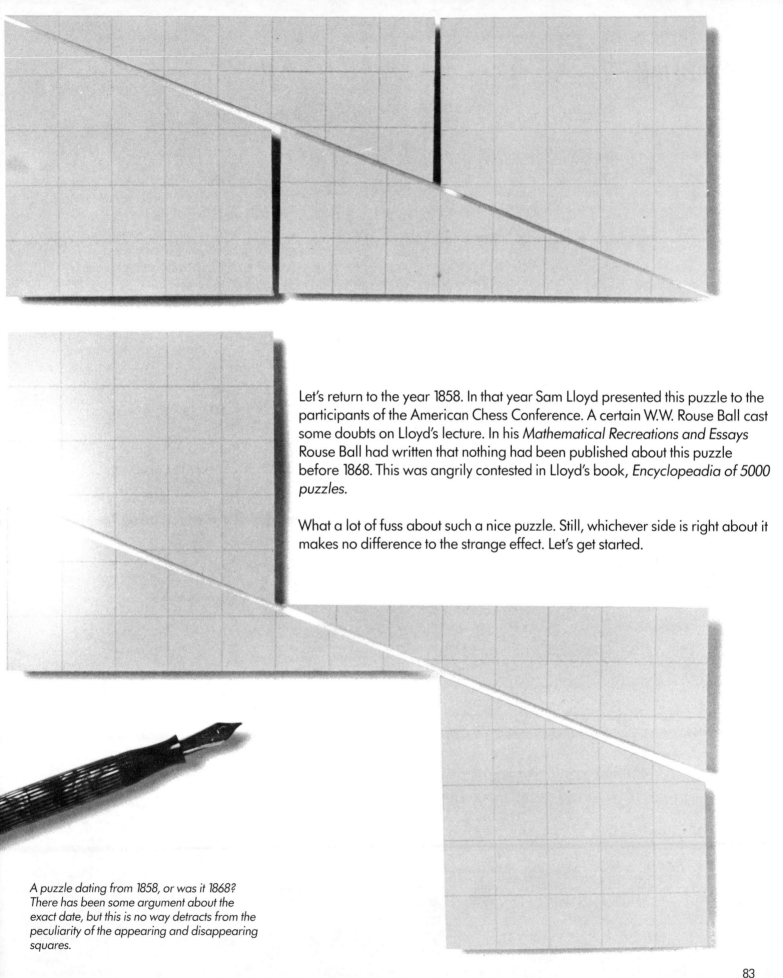

Let's return to the year 1858. In that year Sam Lloyd presented this puzzle to the participants of the American Chess Conference. A certain W.W. Rouse Ball cast some doubts on Lloyd's lecture. In his *Mathematical Recreations and Essays* Rouse Ball had written that nothing had been published about this puzzle before 1868. This was angrily contested in Lloyd's book, *Encyclopeadia of 5000 puzzles.*

What a lot of fuss about such a nice puzzle. Still, whichever side is right about it makes no difference to the strange effect. Let's get started.

A puzzle dating from 1858, or was it 1868? There has been some argument about the exact date, but this is no way detracts from the peculiarity of the appearing and disappearing squares.

GAMBLING 2

The things you can do with dice. You can use them to gamble but you can also play games with them – at least if you make the dice yourself. These games aren't half as childish as they may appear to be at first sight.

Possibly you've already found this in solving the problems from Gambling 1. But if not, try solving this game with dice. Appearances have never been so deceptive as in this brain teaser.

You'll need eight home-made dice and these then have to be piled up in such a way that they form a cube, as well as showing the same number on every side. Be warned again – this is much more difficult than you think. However, your sense of satisfaction will be greatest when you discover the answer to a problem which has almost driven you to despair.

Finally, this octet of dice makes a wonderful present, particularly when the dice are decorated and presented attractively in a box you have made yourself.

The opposite page shows the templates of the eight dice which you have to make for this puzzle. You'll notice that the distribution of the numbers of the various templates differs on all the dice. If possible, use card 0.5 mm thick. To make eight dice you'll need a sheet 50 × 65 cm. This will give you dice measuring 3 × 3 × 3 cm.
Copy the templates onto the sheet of card and draw on the dots as shown in the example. It is absolutely essential to copy these accurately. Remember that you don't always have to draw in the dots. It looks very attractive if stickers are used. Then cut out the templates and score along the fold lines with a Stanley knife. Stick the dice together with glue on the flaps.

If you haven't got enough problems in your life, try tackling this one. It'll help you forget your real troubles.

You'll have to copy the templates of the dice very accurately for the puzzle to work.

Make yourself an alternative to dice. You'll only need some strips of card.
When you've folded this model, you'll have to make two more folds along the dotted line in the direction of the arrow and glue down the last triangle.

HEXAFLEXAGON

We didn't think of this word, so don't blame us. We wouldn't have dared. The word is almost impossible to pronounce – a veritable tongue twister.

It's called a hexaflexagon and this word conceals a surprisingly flexible triangle discovered just before the Second World War by the English student of mathematics, A.H. Stone, who was doing research in the USA. As in most cases of 'great' inventions, the trusty Stone was looking for something quite different – but we won't hold that against him. After all, his discovery has led to a number of amusing puzzles, of which this is just one.

The Hexaflexagon shown here – and we'll try to make that the last time we use the word – consists of nineteen equilateral triangles. Fold all these as shown in the examples on these pages and you'll end up with a hexagon which turns round on its own axis. This is a nice little toy for us, but for Mr A.H. Stone it was merely the first step into the mysterious and amazing world of the Hex...

At first sight this game looks rather complicated to make. But what is complicated? This Hexaflexagon certainly isn't. All you need is a long strip of thick paper or thin card. For the model in our example we've used a strip of card about 40 cm long and 4 cm wide. But provided that you stick to this ratio, you can use any strip as long or as short as you like. Copy the model shown here accurately and score all the fold lines so that all the edges will be as sharp as possible. Then fold the whole thing in the way shown in the example. Make the last folds along the dotted line. As you will see, one of the nineteen triangles will remain, and this triangle can be glued against the opposite triangle.

Now the model is finished, but to make the whole thing more interesting, you could cover it with spots, as in our example, or colour it. If you use the dots

the structure will look like an alternative to dice; if you use colours, make sure you use six different colours.

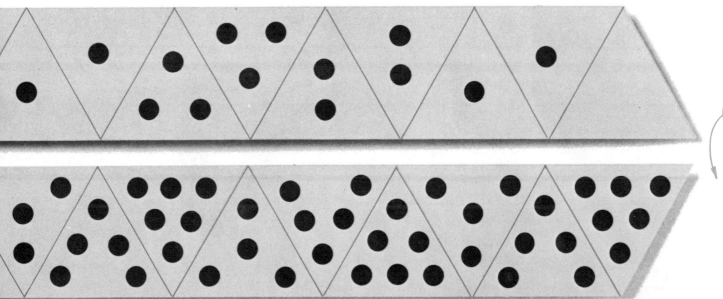

FOLDING, FOLDING

Obviously this is not merely a question of folding simple little squares willy-nilly. In fact, one might suppose that this pastime had some connections with higher mathematics, as well as with art. Certainly paper folding is not a new phenomenon, and the history of this art dates back over two thousand years.

You start with a square of paper divided into sixteen squares with a few dots and cuts here and there. These dots form an awkward but quite amusing problem, ie, to fold the paper in such a way that the squares with the same number of dots come to be opposite each other.

We've made two variations on this puzzle, one of which is simpler than the other. For the first puzzle, divide a piece of paper 10 × 10 cm into sixteen squares. Score along the lines with a Stanley knife and make three grooves in the places shown on the diagram. Fold the paper backwards and forwards along all the lines and show the right number of dots on the model. Dot this exactly according to the example – otherwise attempting the solution to the puzzle will be a hopeless proposition before you even start.

The second puzzle is rather more difficult. This is because of the square hole in the middle. Again it is obviously essential to copy the dots in exactly the right squares.

A puzzle to get your teeth into. You'll alternate between total despair and brief periods of elation. There's no better present you could make for a friend.

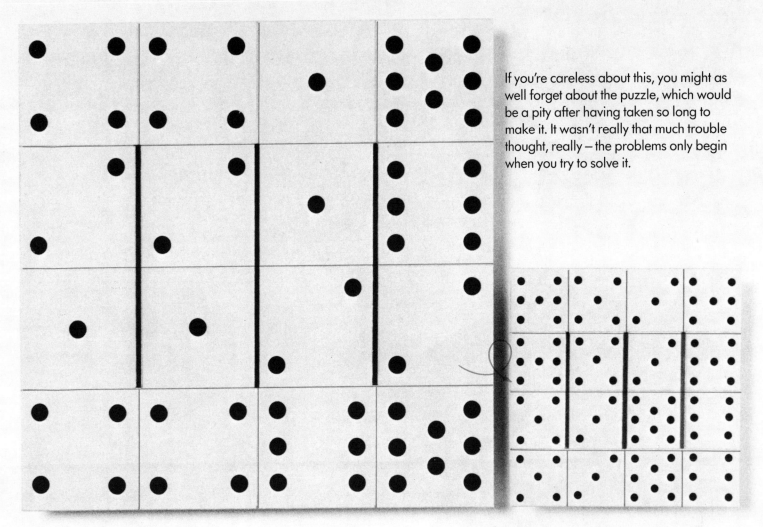

If you're careless about this, you might as well forget about the puzzle, which would be a pity after having taken so long to make it. It wasn't really that much trouble thought, really – the problems only begin when you try to solve it.

Follow the pattern of dots in this example exactly. As you can see, there is a front and a back for most models.

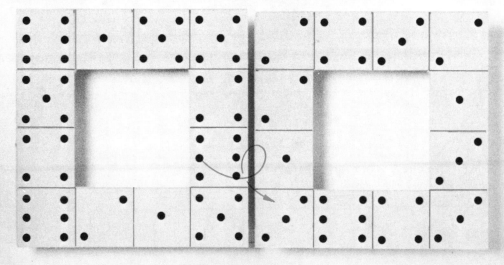

Suggestion. There's a wonderful variation that you could make of the second puzzle. Cut the square 'ring' on one side with a pair of scissors or a Stanley knife and turn it through 180°. Then join it together again with sellotape. You'll soon realize that this makes the puzzle twice as difficult. Whether it also makes the puzzle twice as much fun to do depends entirely on your capacity to persevere.

THE ILLUSION OF REALITY

Don't be afraid to deny that you too have been tricked by this simple illusion. It's an optical joke that we've all played on one another at some time. You take a pencil and a piece of paper and draw two lines exactly the same lenght. One of the lines has arrows at the end pointing inwards and the other has the arrows pointing outwards. The question is: which of the two lines is the longer?

This could be called an optical illusion, and the graphic artist from Leeuwarden, M.C. (Maurits Cornelis) Escher, was a master of this type of optical illusion. In his woodcuts and lithographs he managed to show water running uphill and produced all sorts of other conjuring tricks with perspective that made him world famous.

The designer of the optical illusion shown here was undoubtedly inspired by Escher's work, and you could try copying them in card; at least you could make an attempt, because there are quite a few pitfalls on the way. The two crooked figures below may not be utterly impossible, but what about the figure opposite? Can you dot it or can't you? Is it possible or not? If you can't do it, I'd like to assure you that we managed. Don't give up too quickly. Perhaps we're having you on. Conjuring tricks with perspective are quite fascinating, but sometimes you really feel that your mind is becoming addled.

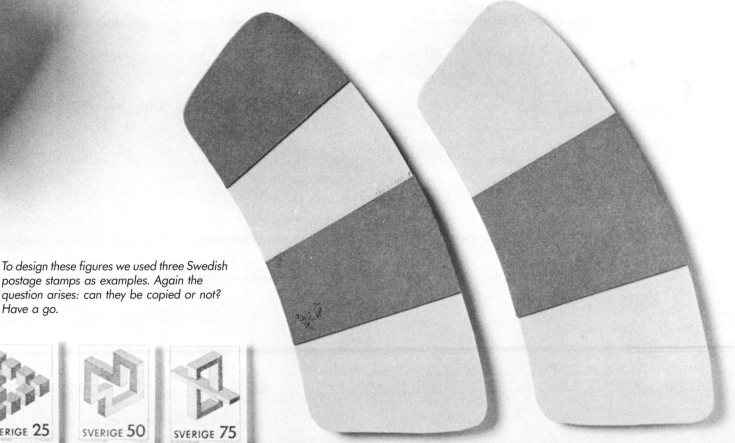

To design these figures we used three Swedish postage stamps as examples. Again the question arises: can they be copied or not? Have a go.

We're not going to tell you how we did it –
we're only going to say that it's actually
possible – or perhaps it isn't.

PICK A NUMBER

In the middle of a conversation, try casually interjecting: 'Hey, guess what I've just found out. I'm clairvoyant.' The chances are that the listeners will immediately demand proof. This won't present any problems. Ask someone to think of a number under sixty and to prevent the others from thinking that it's all a big hoax, he can whisper the number to them.

Now you take out your number cards. These are cards showing a few different numbers. You ask the subject the obvious question: Is the number you're thinking of on this card? If the answer is negative, put the card to one side. If the answer is affirmative, remember the first number on the card. When you've shown your victim all the cards, you have to do some lightning mental arithmetic for you will have to add up all the first numbers on the cards on which the subject saw his secret number. The result of this addition is the number that the subject had in mind. Does this seem rather far-fetched? You might think so at first sight, but it's true and your audience will not discover that you're not really clairvoyant until you tell them the secret. Let them discover it for themselves.

It couldn't be easier to make the strips which you need for this performance. A large piece of card about 1 mm thick is divided into six strips 30 cm long and 3 cm wide. Of course, you can also make them smaller, but if you want to perform to a large audience, it's best not to make the cards too small. Then write down the figures shown here, neatly and clearly on the cards and you're ready for the opening night.

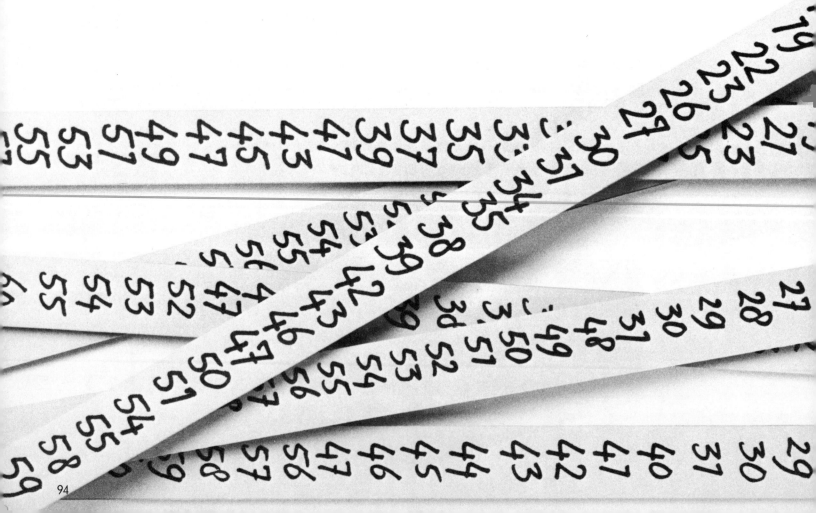

You can use these strips to give a performance as a clairvoyant. Make them now.

Whether you make the strips large or small doesn't really matter, but make sure that you copy the numbers correctly.

Strip 1	Strip 2	Strip 3	Strip 4	Strip 5	Strip 6
1	2	4	8	16	32
3	3	5	9	17	33
5	6	6	10	18	34
7	7	7	11	19	35
9	10	12	12	20	36
11	11	13	13	21	37
13	14	14	14	22	38
15	15	15	15	23	39
17	18	20	24	24	40
19	19	21	25	25	41
21	22	22	26	26	42
23	23	23	27	27	43
25	26	28	28	28	44
27	27	29	29	29	45
29	30	30	30	30	46
31	31	31	31	31	47
33	34	36	40	48	48
35	35	37	41	49	49
37	38	38	42	50	50
39	39	39	43	51	51
41	42	44	44	52	52
43	43	45	45	53	53
45	46	46	46	54	54
47	47	47	47	55	55
49	50	52	56	56	56
51	51	53	57	57	57
53	54	54	58	58	58
55	55	55	59	59	59
57	58	60	60	60	60
59	59				

FLYING WITH PAPER

Building a plane? This art is almost as old as paper itself. There are scores of ways of turning a sheet of paper into all sorts of advanced models of planes. The planes will really fly throught the air for a matter of seconds before crashing down to earth in a graceful arc after a long glide. Usually they crash somewhere you'd never have expected – in the middle of the daffodils, for example, or into the cat's whiskers as it lies dozing in the sun.

Entire books have been devoted to building paper aeroplanes, including *Paper Flight* (David & Charles). We have taken a combination of different planes, together forming a new, futuristic box, though whether this rocket-like toy can really be termed a box is a debatable point. Even real aeroplane builders will find themselves admiring this beautifully assembled model.

For the main body of this plane you'll need a sheet of paper 20 × 30 cm, folded double and then opened out again. Then make two points by folding in the two top corners along the dotted line, and repeat this as shown in the model. Now fold the entire plane double and staple the wings down at the arrow after first pulling them down slightly. Fold the back of the plane back in and up along the dotted line so that there is a so-called 'stabilo'.

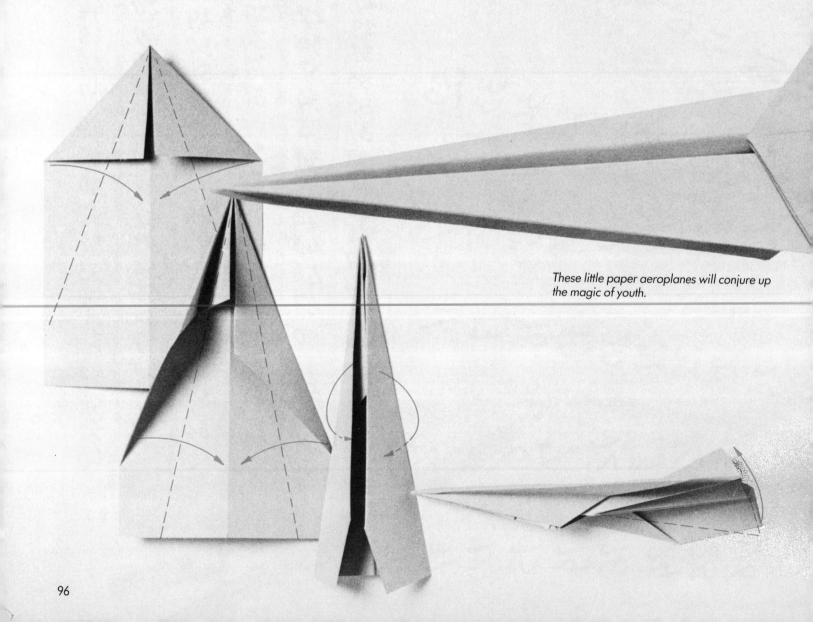

These little paper aeroplanes will conjure up the magic of youth.

Now for the wings. For these you need another sheet of paper 20 × 30 cm. Fold it along the diagonals shown. It's a good idea to fold the paper backwards and forwards a few times.
Now fold the sheet in two lengthways, at the same time pressing in the corners on the diagonals. If you have done this properly, you will see the shape of the wings emerging. Fold the left side, ie, the front of the wing, lightly down and make a small cut in the back, as shown in the example. The four separate points now need to be folded in along the dotted line.

This is a sort of wing in which the top layer is folded straight up at both ends. These are the stabilizers. Now glue the front edge of the wing together. Assemble the whole plane by gluing the main part of the body and the wing together as shown in the example. Ready for take off.

If you want the planes to be really aerodynamic, follow the instructions carefully.

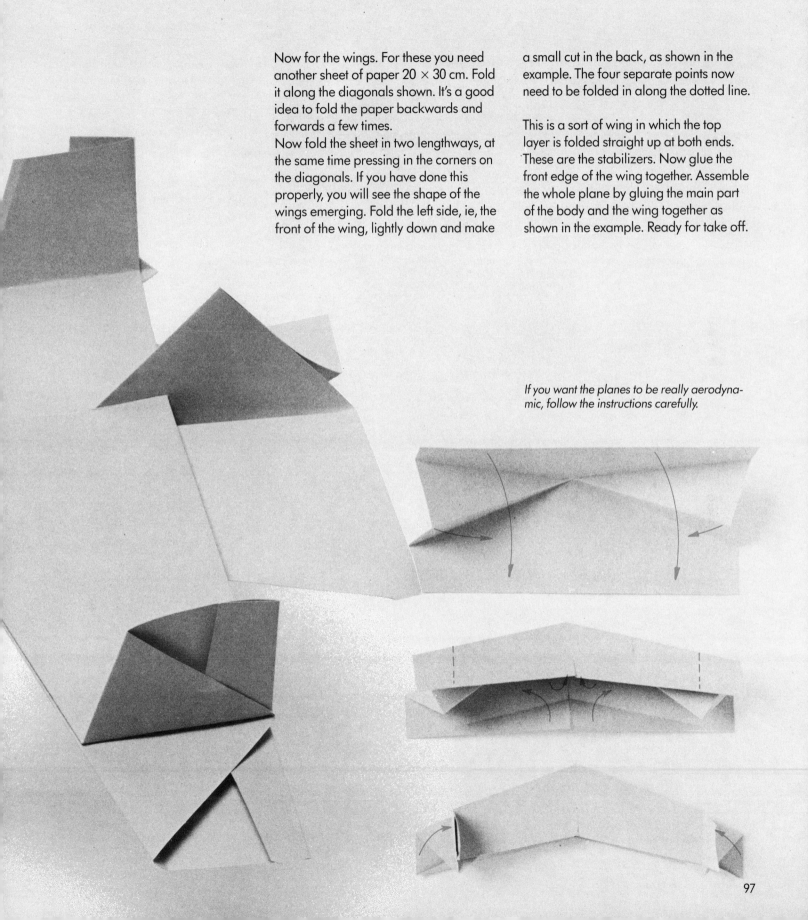

97

MULTIPLES

Multiples are paper aeroplanes which are an absolute delight for any real enthusiast. Ten of these wings are joined together. Try making one yourself. If you get it right you'll produce an unforgettable spectacle. It may sound unbelievable, but you can make these multiples one metre long. Of course, this means you will need six wings or tailpieces, or whatever you choose to call these pieces.

However, the pieces themselves require some description. At first sight the way in which these multiples are constructed looks fairly simple. But the folding instructions must be followed very accuraely – even if you're only a few milli-metres out, your plane will undoubtedly crash to the ground only seconds after you have launched it in the air.

The step-by-step process for making this plane starts with the nose. This is made from a sheet of paper 20 × 20 cm which is first folded along the diagonals. It is also folded widthways at the point where the diagonals intersect. Then fold the whole thing double. No one who has ever built a paper aeroplane before will be surprised that you need to fold the top points down.

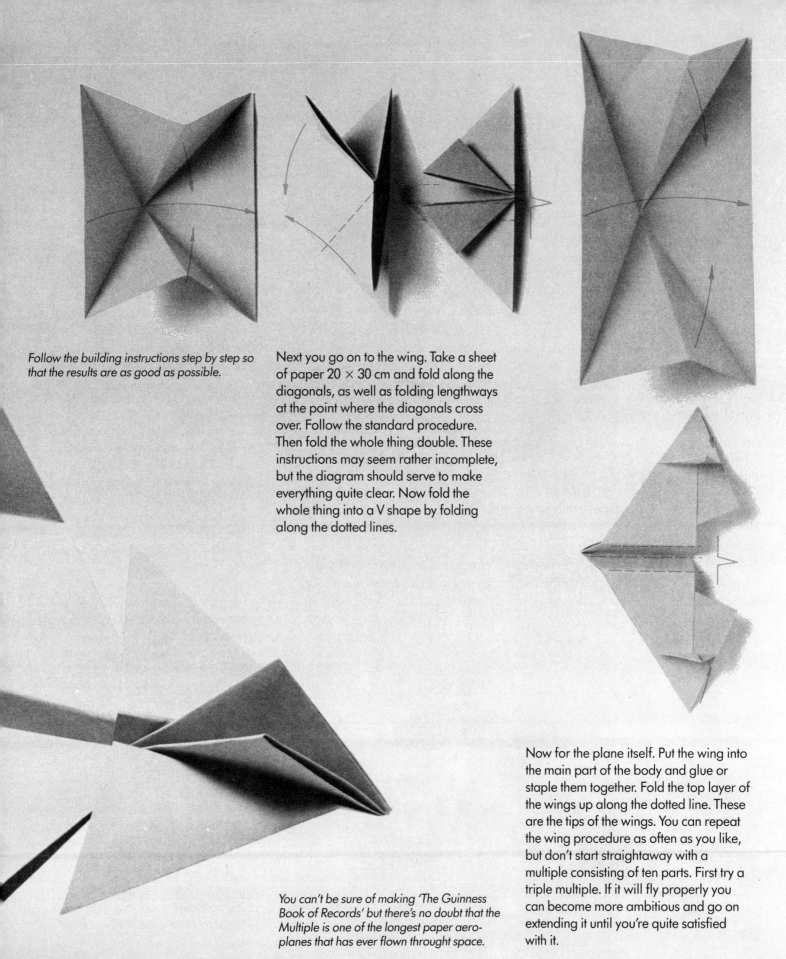

Follow the building instructions step by step so that the results are as good as possible.

Next you go on to the wing. Take a sheet of paper 20 × 30 cm and fold along the diagonals, as well as folding lengthways at the point where the diagonals cross over. Follow the standard procedure. Then fold the whole thing double. These instructions may seem rather incomplete, but the diagram should serve to make everything quite clear. Now fold the whole thing into a V shape by folding along the dotted lines.

You can't be sure of making 'The Guinness Book of Records' but there's no doubt that the Multiple is one of the longest paper aeroplanes that has ever flown throught space.

Now for the plane itself. Put the wing into the main part of the body and glue or staple them together. Fold the top layer of the wings up along the dotted line. These are the tips of the wings. You can repeat the wing procedure as often as you like, but don't start straightaway with a multiple consisting of ten parts. First try a triple multiple. If it will fly properly you can become more ambitious and go on extending it until you're quite satisfied with it.

99

Perhaps some old people will remember these, at least if they have ever been to Paris. Walking along a boulevard, through the evening gloom you would suddenly be terrified to see one of these lifesize silhouettes appearing against a wall some way off. Then when you looked round to see where the giant had suddenly appeared from, you would see a tiny stallholder holding a cardboard cut-out figure between a candle and the wall.

On his stall he would have not only pictures of famous people, but also cut-outs of monsters which could send shivers up your spine when they were projected. In fact, they were really like the negatives of photographs. The stallholder or his supplier would make them by sticking negatives onto a card and cutting out all the black parts.
If these cut-out pieces of card were then held in front of a bright lamp, the image produced on the opposite wall would be greatly enlarged. The black parts of this image were where the cardboard figure created a shadow, and the white parts were where the light shone through the cut-out parts.

If you lit a number of lamps and these were placed behind the cards in different places, there would obviously be a number of different images. In this way you could certainly create a terrifying tableau, particularly with the monster silhouettes. In France this was sometimes known as the 'Danse des Sorciers' ('Dance of the Magicians').

These dancing magicians have disappeared almost entirely from the streets of Paris. It soon became obvious that young ladies doing a striptease were much more interesting than these silhouettes, which were without any sensuality whatsoever.

It may not be particularly difficult to make this sort of figure from a technical point of view, but artistically a little talent is required. The French method of working with negatives doesn't really apply, but there's another method of making a really good phantom.

Make sure you have a bright light, a sheet of paper, a pencil with a sharp point, and some sellotape. Then decide on the 'victim' whom you wish to immortalize with a shadow. Seat this person on a chair about one metre away from the wall and stick the paper onto the wall with sellotape at the level of this person's head.
Now place the bright light on the other side of this person so that a clear black shadow falls onto the paper. You can reduce or enlarge the image by moving the lamp further away or nearer to the victim. With a pencil, draw round the outline of the shadow on the paper and then cut this shape out of the paper so that you have a silhouette.

You may feel quite pleased already, but there's more to come. If you want to make a realistic phantom you must now indicate the features by drawing in where the eyes, mouth, nose etc. should be with the pencil. These are then also cut out.
Don't be surprised if your first attempt is not immediately successful. For this to work really well, you'll have to experiment first. For example, try making some photocopies of photographs in magazines showing portraits of various people. If you examine them with your eyes screwed up, you'll clearly start to recognize the light and dark areas. The light areas have to be cut out, while the dark areas are left.
Once you've practised this a little, you can be confident about trying your first guinea pig on the chair in front of the wall.

With these shadows you can project all sorts
of interesting images onto the wall, particularly
when there are a number of different sources
of light.

SHADOW PLAY 2

In the past there were a number of different theatres in Europe where only galanty shows were performed. Among the most famous were *Le Chat Noir* in France and *Schwabinger Schattenbuhne* in Germany. The latter was founded in about 1910 in the artists' quarter of Munich, Schwabing, by the neo-romantic poets, of whom Alexander von Bernus was the driving force. Artists and musicians were also involved in the company.

The *Schwabinger Schattenbuhne* was situated in a garden house with a rather romantic atmosphere. This atmosphere was further emphasised by music played on a harpsichord. The scenes which were performed had a dream-like character, such as that of *Pan* in which silhouettes glided along a background of soft pastel colours. The images were accompanied by a mysterious voice reading the poems of the above-mentioned von Bernus, and all this contributed to the elevated atmosphere.

The Schwabingers also performed *Grimm's Fairytales* as well as plays based on elements of folklore. The galanty show did not exist for very long, but it did form the basis of the German shadow theatre that was revived after the First World War, because it was rediscovered not only by various youth movements, but also because various art colleges included it in their syllabus.

The great art teacher, Leo Weismantel was one of the first to describe exactly how to make these figures in his book *Schattenspielbuch*. Other shadow artists such as Margarethe Cordes and Annemarie Clochmann also wrote books describing the art of shadow theatre in great detail.

Their figures were often articulated, and sometimes the movements were even joined together. For example, if you moved the left hind leg, the left foreleg would also move. The various parts of this sort of figure would be joined together by narrow hinged pieces of wire or similar material. Thus, by pulling on one lever, various different parts of the figure would move.

The shadow artist, Hede Reidelbach, was incredibly skilled in creating these articulated movements. She made figures in which there were wires at both the front and the back, so that there was an enormous variety of movement.

In the Netherlands, the foremost exponent of shadow theatre, Frans ter Gast, preferred making shadow figures to performing with them, and became well-known throughout Europe. In his performances ter Gast used projection equipment in which the sole source of light was a bicycle lamp. This was connected to a transformer which reduced the voltage from 220 V to 9.3 V. As this sort of bulb usually only takes 6 volts, the voltage was too high and the light was therefore very bright.

Ter Gast was extraordinarily inventive, and this was apparent in the elaborate and sophisticated construction of his figures. For some theatre pieces, such as *Erik*, based on a well-known book by Godfried Bomans, he made shadow figures in which large parts were cut out, and in these he would stick thin coloured paper. These figures were placed in little windows slid into grooves, about 40 cm away from the bulb in the projector.

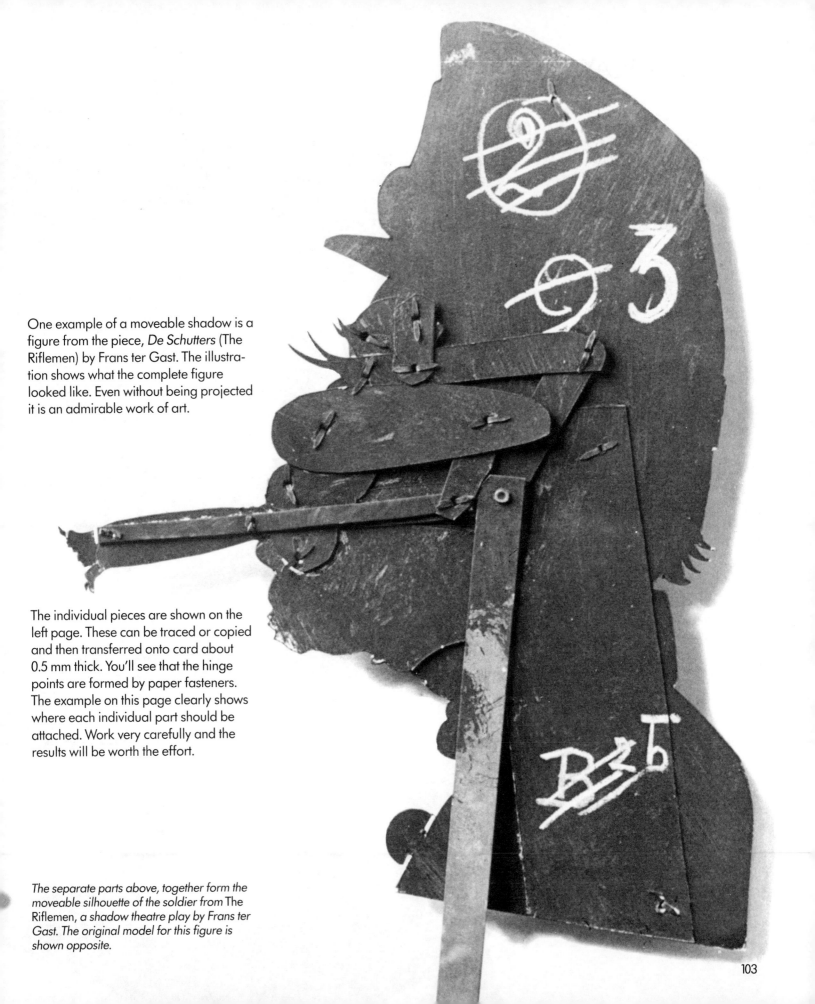

One example of a moveable shadow is a figure from the piece, *De Schutters* (The Riflemen) by Frans ter Gast. The illustration shows what the complete figure looked like. Even without being projected it is an admirable work of art.

The individual pieces are shown on the left page. These can be traced or copied and then transferred onto card about 0.5 mm thick. You'll see that the hinge points are formed by paper fasteners. The example on this page clearly shows where each individual part should be attached. Work very carefully and the results will be worth the effort.

The separate parts above, together form the moveable silhouette of the soldier from The Riflemen, *a shadow theatre play by Frans ter Gast. The original model for this figure is shown opposite.*

SHADOW PLAY 3

In the Netherlands games with shadows suddenly became very popular at the turn of the century. This was due, amongst other things, to the efforts of Ko Doncker from Haarlem, who had a theatre in that city which was often filled to overflowing with spectators, despite its completely delapidated interior. In those days it was absolutely *de rigeur* to have seen Doncker's shows. He was a real joker and a bohemian. He had no scruples about entertaining his rather posh audience with piquant texts and equally spicy pictures. However, Doncker's *outré* productions were acccepted without too many protestations because it was all done in such a humorous way. Doncker also made a shadow tableau for a cigar manufacturer, and this was packaged with the cigars. The cigar magnate was not over-impressed because Doncker's slogan for this tableau was 'Never start smoking too young', hardly the most felicitous slogan for a cigar manufacturer trying to make a profit.

In this tableau Johnny secretly takes a few cigars from his father's cigar box, with obvious consequences. He is as sick as a parrot and makes a fool of himself in class. So he's sent off to the doctor and the doctor gets to work on him. But, alas and alack, poor little Johnny is already an addict. He can't stop smoking. This is all followed by the sad moral of the tale, which is certainly not conducive for smoking cigars:

'Little John would not stop smoking,
   What this led to, you must know,
Huffing, wheezing, puffing, croaking,
   Little John just failed to grow.'

This is a wonderful cartoon shadow story to try and copy, but obviously you can think of something else yourself. To do this you can use pictures from magazines, stick them onto card and then cut them out. Perhaps you'll become a fully fledged 'galanty' artist like Ko Doncker.

SPEL van KO DONCKER "ROOKT NOOIT TE VROEG" 1912

These are the reconstructed shadow figures for Ko Doncker's shadow tableau 'Never Smoke Too Young,' which were sold with cigars at the beginning of this century by way of advertisement. These figures come from the collection of Ger Boonstra.

PYRAMIDS

Folding paper ornaments is a very satisfying way of passing the time. First of all, when you're making them, and later when you decorate the room with them and a visitor makes a flattering remark about your original sculpture. However, there is a disadvantage with some of these home-made works of art: after a while their attraction begins to wear off. It's as though they lose some of their glamour and glitter, and their initial charm is no longer there. Unless, of course, you're such a wonderful artist that your work of art continues to fascinate for years.

However, as we cannot assume that you're a great artist, this is a sculpture that can be given a different face every day. It's a pyramid, which when you inspect closely, appears to consist of a number of small pyramids.
All these small pyramids can be decorated according to your own taste, and can be given a place in the 'mother pyramid' where you think they look best. The effect of this is clear. There are dozens of ways of rearranging the large pyramid to produce a different effect. The pyramid in the example shown here is decorated following the example of Han Makkinga.

An object that can change its face every day.

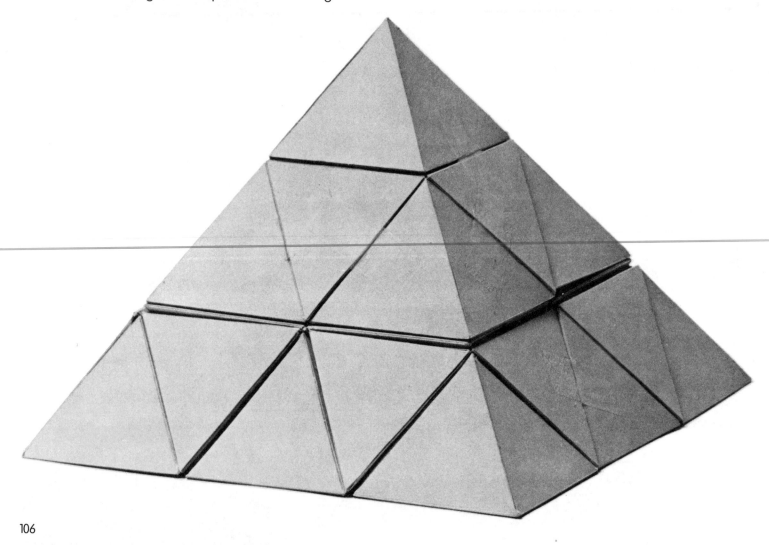

For this work of art you'll need card, glue, sellotape, a knife, a pencil, a ruler and quite a lot of patience. With these you make 19 pyramids with a square base and 16 figures described in a previous chapter as 'tetras'. The diagrams or templates for these are shown below.

Trace the templates onto the card, which should be about 0.5 mm thick. Cut out the templates and score along the fold lines. Glue the pyramids and tetras together with the glue flaps. When all these sections are ready, build the mother pyramid with them.

When making the next step, be very careful. Break the mother pyramid up piece by piece, obviously starting from the top and working down. Join all the small shapes together with sellotape one by one to make a chain. Then 'tattoo' all the small pyramids and tetras with your own design to form a decorative object which you can use as an ornament and possibly also as a beautiful puzzle.

These templates have to be cut out 19 times for the pyramids and 16 times for the tetras.

NOTHING'S IMPOSSIBLE

A popular sentiment amongst older people. In other words, never give up and don't be put off by something that looks impossible at first sight. For example, drawing a portrait of someone without taking the pencil off the paper. There are plenty of examples of this sort of thing. A sentence of many letters which can be read backwards as well as forwards. 'Able was I ere I saw Elba' is a celebrated palindrome.

This folded sculpture is no mean feat to produce. When you've folded it and shown it to someone, they'll never believe it's made from one sheet of paper, but it is. You need only follow the instructions. Just the job for an empty afternoon when the rain is lashing against the windows. The chances are that you'll surprise yourself, because it really does look very strange. How is it possible to create this object from one piece of paper?

Follow this example step by step to produce the completed model.

For this folding structure you need a thick sheet of paper 15 × 12 cm. Draw a pattern of lines on the paper as shown in the diagram below. Remember that the place where the lines end on the side is by no means arbitrary. On the long side this is one third from the corner, and for the short sides it is at one sixth from the corner, ie, in centimetres the lines end at 5 and 2 cm respectively.

The two complete lines are cut; the dotted lines are scored with the blunt edge of a Stanley knife along the folds which have to be made along these lines. Follow the example for the method of folding. When everything is finished, it's a good idea to put two pieces of sellotape at the bottom of the sculpture to ensure that everything stays in place. Now you're ready to amaze your family with this 'impossible' folding sculpture, and you can smugly tell them that nothing's impossible.

You won't believe your eyes, but it's really true. This folding sculpture is made from a single sheet of paper.

By exchanging pieces A and B, one of the
pencils changes colour.

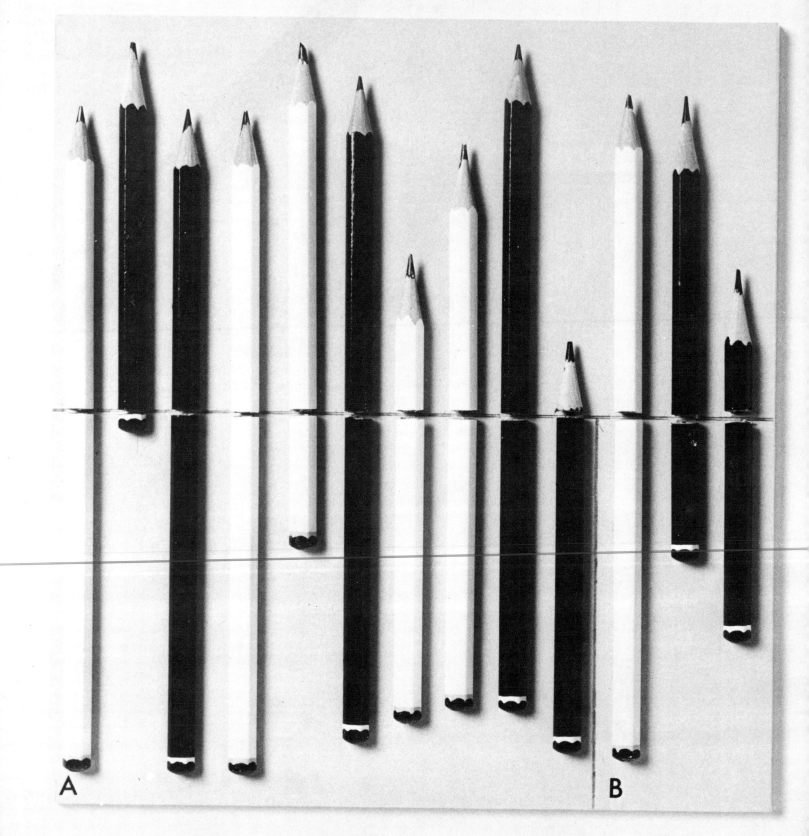

MEL STOVER'S PENCIL

You'll have noticed that you're nearly at the end of the book, so what could be more appropriate than laying your tools on one side, or better still, making them disappear altogether by means of a sophisticated trick. Let's start with the pencils. Get rid of them, preferably in the way invented by Mel Stover.

Mel was a clever chap. When he invented the disappearing pencil trick as long ago as 1956, he immediately patented the idea. Whether this was a great financial success has not been documented, but, after all, for our purposes this is quite unimportant.

The only thing that concerns us is that Mel designed an amusing puzzle for which you'll need thirteen pencils of two colours, six of one colour and seven of another. The pencils should be a particular length, but now that you no longer need them, that should be easy to arrange.

What's this trick all about? With a very simple movement you can make one of these pencils disappear into thin air, and then make it return immediately in another colour. This is what reincarnation is all about. A pencil that had always been black but desperately wanted to be red. Thanks to Mel Stover's ingenuity, here's its big chance.

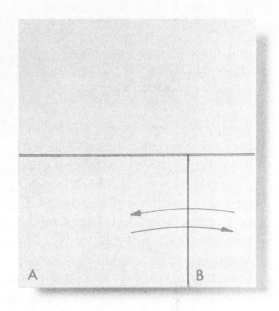

For this trick you'll need a piece of card 20 × 15 cm. Stick the pencils down on this sheet after sawing them exactly to size as shown in the example. You can do this with a small hacksaw or jigsaw, but it's also possible with a Stanley knife. When you've sawn the pencils, stick them down onto the card, which is cut exactly according to the diagram. It should not be even 1 mm out. Obviously the pencils should also be stuck onto the card as shown in the diagram – but you've probably already worked that out for yourself. The strange thing is that when you exchange pieces A and B, one of the pencils changes colour – strange but true.

Cut the card very accurately according to the diagram.
With a simple hacksaw and thirteen old pencils you can perform a miracle in seconds.

THE MAGIC PAPERCLIPS

What's the most succcessful way of telling a joke? It's always best to dress it up a bit. Don't simply drop it into the middle of a conversation, but let it go with the drift of the talk. For example, tell your hairdresser joke when the conversation is about hairdressing ('I was at the hairdresser's yesterday...' etc) and not when you're talking about politics.

When you're performing a trick the same applies. Don't just storm into the dressing room at the football club and shout: 'Look at this boys – I can do a trick!' It's best to wait quietly for the right moment and then come up with your party piece. It should be mentioned that when you do a trick, this should really be a whole performance, so don't rush throught it. The audience won't mind being taken for a ride, but this should always be done as charmingly as possible.

For example, take this trick with paperclips. It's a very simple affair really, which you can do in a couple of seconds with two paperclips, a piece of paper and a deft movement. There's nothing to it. Take a five pound note and fold it in the way shown below, play around with the two paperclips, mumble the magic words, and make a few hand movements until you're sure that everyone's watching, and then pull on the ends of your five pound note.
Hey presto! The paperclips are suddenly joined together. How's it done? There's actually nothing to it. It's a trick that anyone can do, but obviously it won't amount to much without all the accompanying mumbo-jumbo.

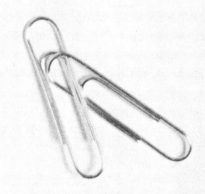

How can you join the paperclips together like this, using only a banknote?

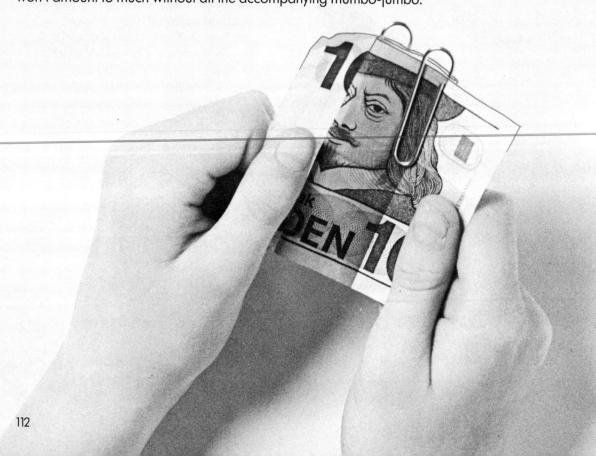

SOLUTIONS

For most puzzles we describe the solution directly after the description. This is necessary for the puzzle to be satisfactorily built. For some of the puzzles (folding puzzles) we do not give a solution, because understanding the explanation will probably be more time-consuming than solving the problem for yourself. As regards the other puzzles, we include the solutions here, but before you look, have a go yourself.

The Divided Chessboard
Pages 18-19

Dudeney's solution.   Brokenshire's solution.   Gary Foshee's solution.

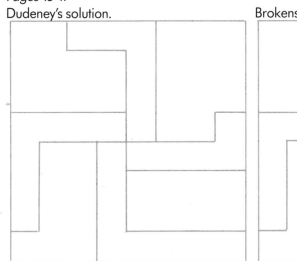

Moving House *Pages 26-27*

3 7 6 4 3 7 6 4 1 A 8 7 6 5 9 2 8 6 A 1
4 7 A 8 6 2 9 5 7 A 8 1 4 A 9 5 7 9 A 4
1 6 8 2 5 A 8 6 1 4 8 3 9 7 A 6 8 3 7 A
60 actions.

1	A		2
6	7	8	9
4	3		5

Catching The Swan

7 5 6 ⌄ 2 3 ⌄ 1 4 2 3 ⌃
1 4 2 3 Z 7 5 6 1 4 3
2 Z 7 5 6 1 7 5 6 1 7 4 2 ⌄ Z 5 6 ⌄ 4 2 ⌄
3 Z
7 1 4 6 ↙ 4 7 2 3 1
49 actions.

1	2	3
4	5	6
Z		7

⌄ Down
⌃ To the Left
↙ ↘ Turn Left, Turn Right

113

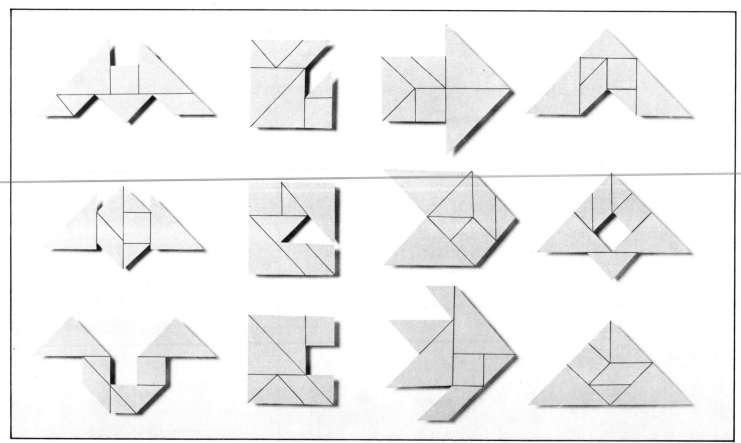

Tangram
Pages 36-37

Matchboxes by Van Deventer
Pages 38-39
One of the three solutions to this puzzle.
Thank you Oskar.

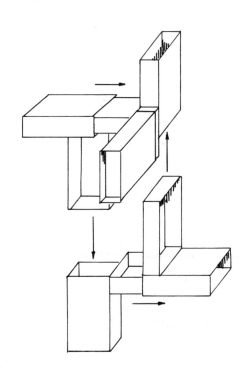

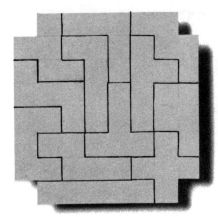

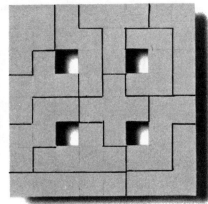

Pentominos
Pages 45-47
Naturally not only these solutions apply.
For each puzzle there are at least two, to
a maximum of over one thousand.

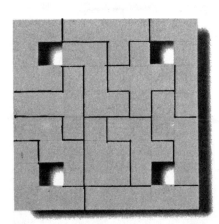

Gambling 1

Pages 52-53

This drawing gives you the solution to this problem. The numbers indicate the result on page 53.

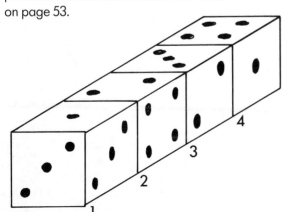

Gambling 2

Pages 84-85

And now look for the solution. Place the following pieces so that each side of the cube shows 4 different numbers.

They made this book (from left to right):
Rob van den Dobbelsteen, Jack Botermans,
David van Dijk and Jeannet Leendertse.

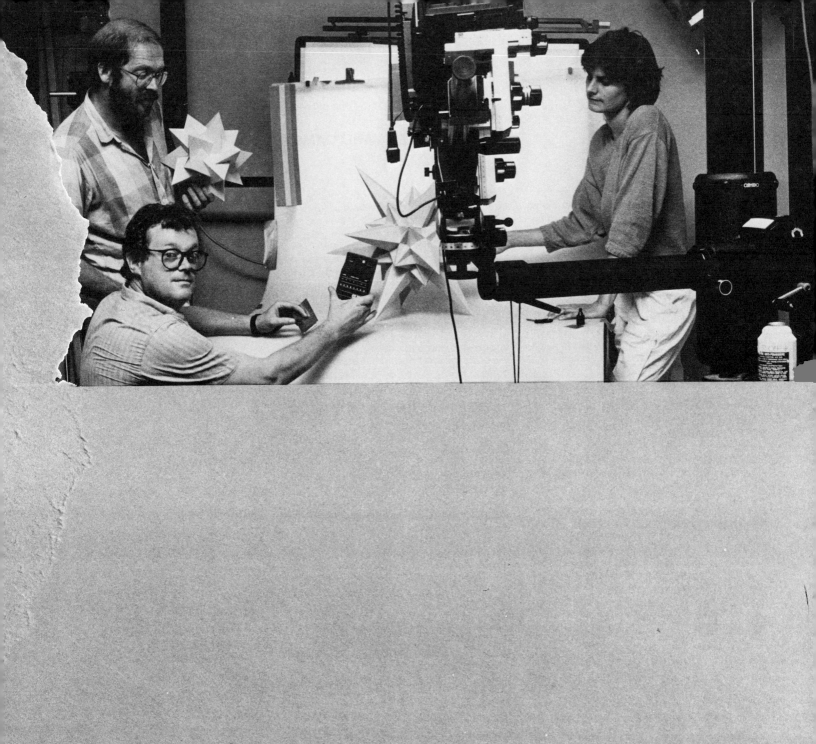

Also available from David & Charles

PAPER FLIGHT
48 models ready for take-off
Jack Botermans

Take one piece of paper, fold it following the clear step-by-step instructions and illustrations, and in no time your own model will be gliding and swooping through the air. The whole family will love making these expertly designed paper flyers – whether of famous aircraft such as the Mirage jet or the Tiger Moth, improvised ones like the Wright Brothers plane, experimental models of flying saucers or helicopters, or fighters like the Cirrus 75 or the Hunter. Moving to the world's natural aerobats, there are model birds like the crane, the heron or the eagle, and remarkably lifelike models of a dragonfly, a moth and other insects.

CALLIGRAPHY NOW
New Light on Traditional Letters
Margaret Shepherd

Clear and exciting information about the most avant-garde aspects of calligraphy today – for the experienced calligrapher wondering what to try next, or for the beginner wondering where to start. Margaret Shepherd's seventh book places modern calligraphy firmly in the traditions of the past, and offers a glimpse of the future. There are simple instructions and lucid drawings, clear alphabet models to copy, plenty of suggested projects and lists of inexpensive materials. With this advice, the calligrapher will gain a full understanding of contemporary letters, and learn how to write them beautifully.

WOODEN PUZZLES AND GAMES
Intriguing projects you can make
Kenneth Wells

The widespread interest in crafts, and the equally extensive fascination with all kinds of puzzles and games, suggest that the time is ripe for a book of mainly traditional wooden puzzles and games adapted to appeal to the craftsman of today. Many of the projects in this book have been familiar for hundreds, if not thousands, of years. Carefully made of good quality materials, they will not only provide pleasure today – plus a good bit of frustration! – but could well become the collector's items of tomorrow. Profusely illustrated with step-by-step photographs and line drawings, this book will soon become an essential addition to any woodworker's library.

MAKING MOVING WOODEN TOYS
Anthony and Judy Peduzzi

Everyone loves brightly-painted wooden toys; they are streng, long lasting, cheerful and fun, and give hours of pleasure to both children and adults. The authors are full-time toymakers who have, over the years, built up a vast collection of moving wooden toys. The fifteen easily made projects in this book can all be constructed using the minimum amount of woodworking equipment and skill, and are suitable for those working at home, or in school or college. The instructions are straightforward and simple, the projects are wonderfully varied and illustrated in colour photographs.
An added bonus is that the toys are suitable for mentally and physically handicapped people, as only a very slight action is required to set them in motion.